Workshop on Grammar Engineering Across Framework 2009

(GEAF 2009)

Held at ACL-IJCNLP 2009

Singapore
6 August 2009

ISBN: 978-1-61738-447-9

Printed from e-media with permission by:

Curran Associates, Inc.
57 Morehouse Lane
Red Hook, NY 12571

Some format issues inherent in the e-media version may also appear in this print version.

Printed by Curran Associates, Inc. (2010)

For permission requests, please contact the Association for Computational Linguistics at the address below.

Association for Computational Linguistics
209 N. Eighth Street
Stroudsburg, Pennsylvania 18360

Phone: 1-570-476-8006
Fax: 1-570-476-0860

acl@aclweb.org

Additional copies of this publication are available from:

Curran Associates, Inc.
57 Morehouse Lane
Red Hook, NY 12571 USA
Phone: 845-758-0400
Fax: 845-758-2634
Email: curran@proceedings.com
Web: www.proceedings.com

Organizers:

Tracy Holloway King, Microsoft
Marianne Santaholma, Geneva University

Program Committee:

Emily Bender, University of Washington (USA)
Miriam Butt, Universität Konstanz (Germany)
John Carroll, University of Sussex (UK)
Stephen Clark, University of Cambridge (UK)
Ann Copestake, University of Cambridge (UK)
Berthold Crysmann, Universität Bonn (Germany)
Mary Dalrymple, University of Oxford (UK)
Stefanie Dipper, Universität Bochum (Germany)
Dan Flickinger, Stanford University (USA)
Josef van Genabith, Dublin City University (Ireland)
Julia Hockenmaier, University of Illinois (USA)
Ron Kaplan, Microsoft (USA)
Montserrat Marimon, Universitat de Barcelona (Spain)
Gertjan van Noord, University of Groningen (The Netherlands)
Jun'ichi Tsujii, University of Tokyo (Japan) / Univeristy of Manchester (UK)

Table of Contents

Conference Program

Thursday, 6 August 2009

Session 1

8:30–9:00 *Exploration of the LTAG-Spinal Formalism and Treebank for Semantic Role Labeling*
Yudong Liu and Anoop Sarkar

9:00–9:30 *Developing German Semantics on the basis of Parallel LFG Grammars*
Sina Zarrieß

9:30–10:00 *Mining of Parsed Data to Derive Deverbal Argument Structure*
Olga Gurevich and Scott Waterman

10:00–10:30 Break

Demo Session (with quick fire presentations)

10:30–12:10 *Parallel Grammar Engineering for Slavic Languages*
Tania Avgustinova and Yi Zhang
HaG — An HPSG of Hausa
Berthold Crysmann
EGAD: Erroneous Generation Analysis and Detection
Michael Goodman and Francis Bond
Deverbal Nouns in a Semantic Search Application
Olga Gurevich, Scott A. Waterman, Dick Crouch and Tracy Holloway King
A Web-interface for Eliciting Lexical Type of New Lexemes
Joshua Hou

12:10-13:30 Lunch

Session 2

13:30–14:00 *Autosegmental representations in an HPSG of Hausa*
Berthold Crysmann

14:00–14:30 *Construction of a German HPSG grammar from a detailed treebank*
Bart Cramer and Yi Zhang

14:30–15:00 *Parenthetical Constructions - an Argument against Modularity*
Eva Banik

15:00–15:30 *Using Artificially Generated Data to Evaluate Statistical Machine Translation*
Manny Rayner, Paula Estrella, Pierrette Bouillon, Beth Ann Hockey and Yukie Nakao

15:30–16:00 Break

Thursday, 6 August 2009 (continued)

Session 3

16:00–16:30 *Using Large-scale Parser Output to Guide Grammar Development*
Ascander Dost and Tracy Holloway King

16:30–17:00 *A generalized method for iterative error mining in parsing results*
Daniël de Kok, Jianqiang Ma and Gertjan van Noord

17:00-18:00 **Discussion Session**
Moderator: Joakim Nivre

Exploration of the LTAG-Spinal Formalism and Treebank for Semantic Role Labeling

Yudong Liu and **Anoop Sarkar**
School of Computing Science
Simon Fraser University
{yudongl,anoop}@cs.sfu.ca

Abstract

LTAG-spinal is a novel variant of traditional Lexicalized Tree Adjoining Grammar (LTAG) introduced by (Shen, 2006). The LTAG-spinal Treebank (Shen et al., 2008) combines elementary trees extracted from the Penn Treebank with Propbank annotation. In this paper, we present a semantic role labeling (SRL) system based on this new resource and provide an experimental comparison with CCGBank and a state-of-the-art SRL system based on Treebank phrase-structure trees. Deep linguistic information such as predicate-argument relationships that are either implicit or absent from the original Penn Treebank are made explicit and accessible in the LTAG-spinal Treebank, which we show to be a useful resource for semantic role labeling.

1 Introduction

Semantic Role Labeling (SRL) aims to identify and label all the arguments for each predicate in a sentence. Specifically, it involves identifying portions of the sentence that represent the predicate's arguments and assigning pre-specified semantic roles to them.

[$\text{A0}_{\text{seller}}$ *Ports of Call Inc.*] reached agreements to [V_{verb} *sell*] [A1_{thing} *its remaining seven aircraft*] [A2_{buyer} *to buyers that weren't disclosed*] .

is an example of SRL annotation from the PropBank corpus (Palmer et al., 2005), where the subscripted information maps the semantic roles A0, A1 and A2 to arguments for the predicate *sell* as defined in the PropBank Frame Scheme.

The availability of annotated corpora like PropBank and FrameNet (Fillmore et al., 2001) have provided rapid development of research into SRL (Gildea and Jurafsky, 2002; Gildea and Palmer, 2002; Surdeanu et al., 2003; Chen and Rambow, 2003; Gildea and Hockenmaier, 2003; Xue and Palmer, 2004; Pradhan et al., 2004; Pradhan et al., 2005). The shared tasks in CoNLL-2004 (Carreras and Màrquez, 2004), CoNLL-2005 (Carreras and Màrquez, 2005) and CoNLL-2008 (Surdeanu et al., 2008) were all focused on SRL.

SRL systems (Gildea and Jurafsky, 2002; Gildea and Palmer, 2002) have extensively used features defined over Penn Treebank phrase-structure trees. Other syntactic representations such as CCG derivations (Gildea and Hockenmaier, 2003) and dependency trees (Hacioglu, 2004; Surdeanu et al., 2008) have also been explored. It has been previously noted that LTAG, which has the useful property of *extended domain of locality* (EDL), is well-suited to address the SRL task, c.f. (Chen and Rambow, 2003; Liu and Sarkar, 2007). However, LTAG elementary trees were extracted from the derived parse trees by using Magerman-Collins style head-percolation based heuristic rules (Liu and Sarkar, 2007). The LTAG-spinal Treebank (Shen et al., 2008) provided a corpus of derivation trees where elementary trees were extracted from the Penn Treebank in combination with the Propbank predicate-argument annotation. The LTAG-spinal Treebank can be used to overcome some of the limitations of the previous work on SRL using LTAG: (Liu and Sarkar, 2007) uses LTAG-based features extracted from phrase-structure trees as an additional source of features and combined them with features from a phrase-structure based SRL framework; (Chen and Rambow, 2003) only considers those complement/adjunct semantic roles that can be localized in LTAG elementary trees, which leads to a loss of over 17% instances of semantic roles even from gold-standard trees.

The LTAG-spinal formalism was initially proposed for automatic treebank extraction and statistical parsing (Shen and Joshi, 2005). However, its Propbank-guided treebank extraction process further strengthens the connection between the LTAG-spinal and semantic role labeling. In this paper, we present an SRL system that was built to

Proceedings of the 2009 Workshop on Grammar Engineering Across Frameworks, ACL-IJCNLP 2009, pages 1–9,
Suntec, Singapore, 6 August 2009.

explore the utility of this new formalism, its Treebank and the output of its statistical parser. Experiments show that our LTAG-spinal based SRL system achieves very high precision on both gold-standard and automatic parses, and significantly outperforms the one using CCGbank. More importantly, it shows that LTAG-spinal is an useful resource for semantic role labeling, with the potential for further improvement.

2 LTAG-spinal, its Treebank and Parsers

This section gives a brief introduction of LTAG-spinal formalism, its Treebank that is extracted with the help of Propbank annotation, and its two statistical parsers that are trained on the Treebank. Predicate-argument relations encoded in the LTAG-spinal treebank will also be discussed to illustrate its compatibility with Propbank and their potential utility for the SRL task.

2.1 LTAG-spinal

The LTAG-spinal formalism (Shen et al., 2008) is a variant of Lexicalized Tree Adjoining Grammar (LTAG) (Abeillé and Rambow, 2001). Compared to traditional LTAG, the two types of elementary trees (e-tree for short), initial and auxiliary trees, are in *spinal* form with no substitution nodes for arguments appearing in the predicate e-tree: a spinal initial tree is composed of a *lexical spine* from the root to the anchor, and nothing else; a spinal auxiliary tree is composed of a *lexical spine* and a *recursive spine* from the root to the foot node. For example, in Figure 1 (from (Shen et al., 2008)), the lexical spine for the auxiliary tree is $B_1, .., B_i, .., B_n$, the recursive spine is $B_1, .., B_i, .., B_1^*$. Two operations *attachment* and *adjunction* are defined in LTAG-spinal where adjunction is the same as adjunction in the traditional LTAG; attachment stems from *sister adjunction* as defined in Tree Insertion Grammar (TIG) (Schabes and Shieber, 1994), which corresponds to the case where the root of an initial tree is taken as a child of another spinal e-tree. The two operations are applied to LTAG-spinal e-tree pairs resulting in an LTAG derivation tree which is similar to a dependency tree (see Figure 2). In Figure 2, e-tree anchored with *continue* is the only auxiliary tree; all other e-trees are initial trees. The arrow is directed from parent to child, with the type of operation labeled on the arc. The operation types are: *att* denotes *attachment* operation; *adj* denotes *adjunction* operation. The sibling nodes may have different landing site along the parent spine. For example, among the child nodes of *stabilize* e-tree, *to* e-tree has VP as landing site; while *even* has S as landing site. Such information, on some level, turns out to be helpful to differentiate the semantic role played by the different child nodes.

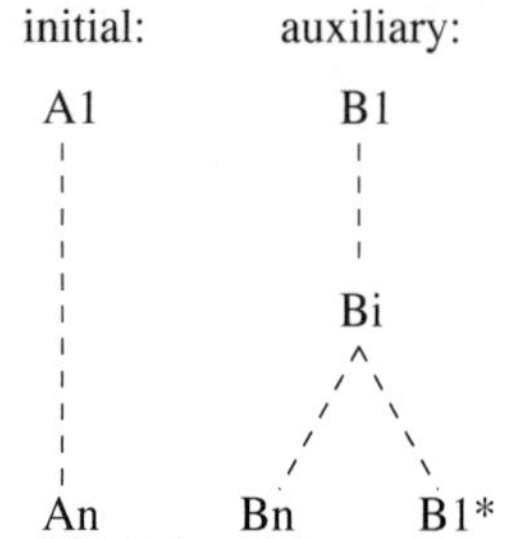

Figure 1: Spinal elementary trees

So far, we can see that in contrast with traditional LTAG where arguments refer to obligatory constituents only, subcategorization frames and argument-adjunct distinction are underspecified in LTAG-spinal. Since argument-adjunct disambiguation is one of the major challenges faced by LTAG treebank construction, LTAG-spinal works around this issue by leaving the disambiguation task for further deep processing, such as semantic role labeling.

LTAG-spinal is weakly equivalent to traditional LTAG with adjunction constraints[1] (Shen, 2006).

The Propbank (Palmer et al., 2005) is an annotated corpus of verb subcategorization and alternations which was created by adding a layer of predicate-argument annotation over the phrase structure trees in the Penn Treebank. The LTAG-spinal Treebank is extracted from the Penn Treebank by exploiting Propbank annotation. Specifically, as described in (Shen et al., 2008), a Penn Treebank syntax tree is taken as an LTAG-spinal derived tree; then information from the Penn Treebank and Propbank is merged using tree transformations. For instance, LTAG predicate coordination and instances of adjunction are recognized using Propbank annotation. LTAG elementary trees are then extracted from the transformed Penn Treebank trees recursively, using the Propbank annotation and a Magerman-Collins style head percolation table.

This guided extraction process allows syntax and semantic role information to be combined in LTAG-spinal derivation trees. For example, the

[1] null adjunction (NA), obligatory adjunction (OA) and selective adjunction (SA)

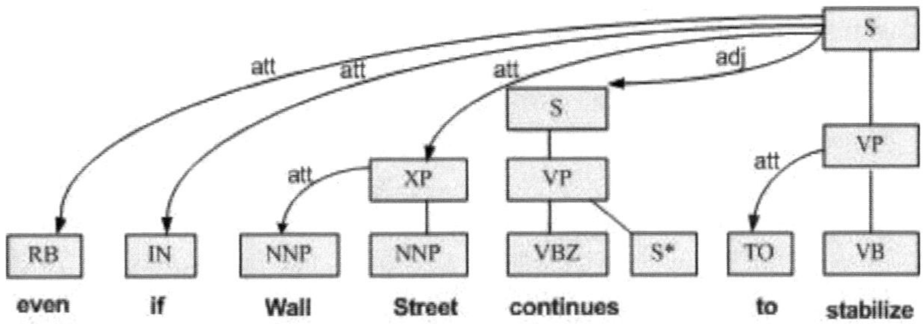

Figure 2: An example of LTAG-spinal sub-derivation tree, from LTAG-spinal Treebank Section 22

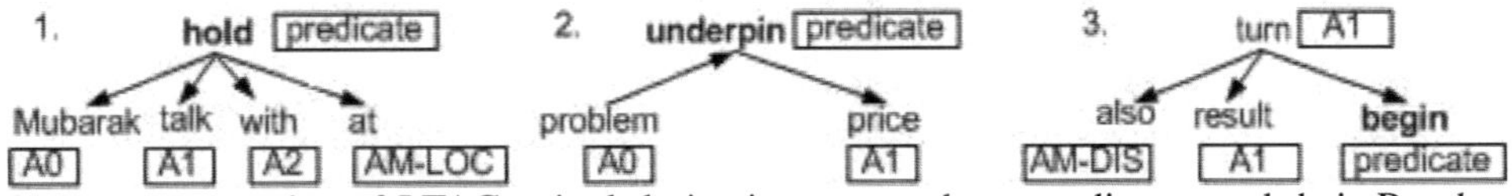

Figure 3: Three examples of LTAG-spinal derivation trees where predicates and their Propbank style argument labels are given. These examples are from LTAG-spinal Treebank Section 22.

Penn Treebank does not differentiate raising verbs and control verbs, however, based on the Propbank information, LTAG-spinal makes this distinction explicit. Thus, the error of taking a subject argument which is not semantically an argument of the raising verb can be avoided. Another property of LTAG-spinal Treebank extraction lies in the flexibility and simplicity of the treatment of predicate coordination (see (Shen et al., 2008)). Figure 3 shows three examples of Propbank annotation as decorations over the LTAG-spinal derivation trees. In each derivation tree, each node is associated with LTAG-spinal e-trees. Each argument (A0, A1, etc.) is referred to as A and the predicate is called P. In most cases, the argument is found locally in the derivation tree due to the extended domain of locality in e-trees. Thus, most arguments are identified by the pattern $P \rightarrow A$ or $P \leftarrow A$. The next section contains a discussion of such patterns in more detail.

Two statistical parsers have been developed by Libin Shen specifically for training on the LTAG-spinal treebank: a left-to-right incremental parser (Shen and Joshi, 2005) and a bidirectional incremental parser (Shen and Joshi, 2008). If one compares the output of these two parsers, the left-to-right parser produces full LTAG-spinal derivation trees (including all the information about specific elementary trees used in the derivation and the attachment information within the e-trees) while the bidirectional parser produces derivation trees without information about elementary trees or attachment points (similar to output from a dependency parser). In this paper, we use the left-to-right incremental parser for its richer output because our SRL system uses feature functions that use information about the elementary trees in the derivation tree and the attachment points between e-trees. The landing site of child node along the parent spine is useful for identifying different types of arguments in SRL. For example, assume the parent spine is "S-VP-VB-anchor" (the root label is S, and "anchor" is where the lexical item is inserted). Along with direction information, the landing site label "S" is likely to be a good indicator for argument A0 (subject) while the landing site label "VP" could be a good indicator for "A1" (object). In this sense, the incremental left-to-right parser is preferable for semantic role labeling. However, having been developed earlier than the bidirectional parser, the incremental parser obtains 1.2% less in dependency accuracy compared to the bidirectional parser (Shen and Joshi, 2008).

2.2 Predicate-argument relations in the LTAG-spinal Treebank

The Propbank-guided extraction process for LTAG-spinal treebank naturally creates a close connection between these two resources. To examine the compatibility of the LTAG-spinal Treebank with Propbank, (Shen et al., 2008) provides the frequency for specific types of paths from the predicate to the argument in the LTAG-spinal derivation trees from the LTAG-spinal Treebank. The 8 most frequent patterns account for 95.5% of the total predicate-argument pairs of the LTAG-spinal Treebank, of which 88.4% are directly connected pairs. These statistics not only provide em-

	Path Pattern	Number	Percent
1	P→A	8294	81.3
2	P←A, V←A	720	7.1
3	P←Px→A	437	4.3
4	P←Coord→Px→A	216	2.1
5	P←Ax←Py→A	84	0.82
6	P←Coord←Px→A	40	0.39
7	P←Px←Py→A	13	0.13
total recovered w/ patterns		9804	96.1
total		10206	100.0

Table 1: Distribution of the 7 most frequent predicate-argument pair patterns in LTAG-spinal Treebank Section 22. P: predicate, A: argument, V: modifying verb, $Coord$: predicate coordination.

pirical justification for the notion of the extended domain of locality (EDL) in LTAG-spinal (Shen et al., 2008), they also provide motivation to explore this Treebank for the SRL task.

We collected similar statistics from Treebank Section 22 for the SRL task, shown in Table 1, where 7 instead of 8 patterns suffice in our setting. Each pattern describes one type of P(redicate)-A(rgument) pair with respect to their dependency relation and distance in the LTAG-spinal derivation tree. The reason that we combine the two patterns P←A and V←A into one is that from SRL perspective, they are equivalent in terms of the dependency relation and distance between the predicate. Each token present in the patterns, such as P, Px, Py, V, A, Ax and Coord, denotes a spinal e-tree in the LTAG-spinal derivation tree.

To explain the patterns more specifically, take the LTAG-spinal sub-derivation tree in Figure 2 as an example, Assume P(redicate) in question is *stabilize* then (*stabilize* → *even*), (*stabilize* → *if*), (*stabilize* → *Street*), (*stabilize* → *continue*), (*stabilize* → *to*) all belong to pattern 1; but only (*stabilize* → *Street*) is actual predicate-argument pair. Similarly, when take *continue* as P, the predicate-argument pair (*continue* ← *stabilize*) belongs to pattern 2, where *stabilize* corresponds to A(rgument) in the pattern; (*continue*, *Street*) in (*Street* ← *stabilize* → *continue*) is an example of pattern 3, where *stabilize* corresponds to Px and *Street* corresponds to A in the pattern 3 schema. Pattern 4 denotes the case where argument (A) is shared between coordinated predicates (P and Px); The main difference of pattern 5-7 exists where the sibling node of A(rgument) is categorized into: predicate (Px) in pattern 7, predicate coordination node (Coord) in pattern 6 and others (Ax) in pattern 5. We will retain this difference instead of merging it since the semantic relation between P and A varies based on these differences. Example sentences for other (rarer) patterns can be found in (Shen et al., 2008).

3 LTAG-spinal based SRL System Description

In this section, we describe our LTAG-spinal based SRL system. So far, we have studied LTAG-spinal formalism, its treebank and parsers. In particular, the frequency distribution of the seven most seen predicate-argument pair patterns in LTAG-spinal Treebank tells us that predicate-argument relationships typical to semantic role labeling are often local in LTAG-spinal derivation trees.

Pruning, argument identification and argument classification – the 3-stage architecture now standard in SRL systems is also used in this paper. Specifically, for the sake of efficiency, nodes with high probability of being NULL (non-argument) should be filtered at the beginning; usually filtering is done based on some heuristic rules; after the pruning stage, argument identification takes place with the goal of classifying the pruning-survival nodes into argument and non-argument; for those nodes that have been classified as arguments, argument classification component will further label them with different argument types, such as A0, A1, etc. Argument identification and classification are highly ambiguous tasks and are usually accomplished using a machine learning method.

For our LTAG-spinal based SRL system, we first collect the argument candidates for each predicate from the LTAG-spinal derivation tree. For each candidate, features are extracted to capture the predicate-argument relations. Binary classifiers for identification and classification are trained using SVMs and combined in a one-vs-all model. The results are evaluated using precision/recall/f-score.

3.1 Candidate Locations for Arguments

In SRL systems that perform role labeling of constituents in a phrase-structure tree, statistics show that after pruning, ∼98% of the SRL argument nodes are retained in the gold-standard trees in the Penn Treebank, which provides a high upper-bound for the recall of the SRL system. Pruning away unnecessary nodes using a heuristic makes learning easier as well, as many of the false positives are pruned away leading to a more balanced binary classification problem during the semantic role identification and classification steps. We need a similar heuristic over LTAG-spinal nodes that will have high coverage with respect to SRL arguments and provide a high upper-bound for recall.

As previously shown that the seven most frequent predicate-argument pair patterns that are used to describe the specific types of paths from the predicate to the argument account for ~96% of the total number of predicate-argument pairs in the LTAG-spinal Treebank. These patterns provide a natural candidate selection strategy for our SRL.

Table 2 shows a similar oracle test applied to the output of the LTAG-spinal parser on Section 22. The total drop in oracle predicate-argument identifiation drops 10.5% compared to gold-standard trees. 9.8% is lost from patterns 1 and 2. If exclude those pairs that belong to pattern i in treebank but belong to pattern j ($i \neq j$) in automatic parses (so the pattern exists but is the wrong one for that constituent), the number drops to 81.6% from 85.6%. This indicates that in terms of the impact of the syntactic parser errors for SRL, the LTAG-spinal parser will suffer even more than the phase structure parser. An alternative is to exhaustively search for predicate-argument pairs without considering patterns, which we found introduces too much noise in the learner to be feasible. Thus, the predicate-argument pairs selected through this phase are considered as argument candidates for our SRL system.

3.2 Features

Based on the patterns, features are defined on predicate-argument pairs from LTAG derivation tree, mainly including *predicate e-trees*, *argument e-trees*, *intermediate e-trees* and their "topological relationships" such as *operation, spine node, relative position* and *distance*. The following are the specific features used in our classifiers:

	Path Pattern	Number	Percent
1	P→A	7441	72.9
2	P←A, V←A	583	5.7
3	P←Px→A	384	3.8
4	P←Coord→Px→A	180	1.76
5	P←Ax←Py→A	75	0.73
6	P←Coord←Px→A	48	0.47
7	P←Px←Py→A	22	0.21
total recovered w/ patterns		8733	85.6
total		10206	100.0

Table 2: Distribution of the 7 patterns in LTAG-spinal parser output for Section 22.

Features from predicate e-tree and its variants predicate lemma, POS tag of predicate, predicate voice, spine of the predicate e-tree, 2 variants of predicate e-tree: replacing anchor in the spine with predicate lemma, replacing anchor POS in the spine with voice. In Figure 2, if take *stabilize* as predicate, these two variants are *S-VP-VB-stabilize* and *S-VP-VB-active* respectively.

Features from argument e-tree and its variants argument lemma, POS tag of argument, Named Entity (NE) label of the argument, spine of the argument e-tree, 2 variants of argument e-tree: replacing anchor in the spine with argument lemma, replacing anchor POS with NE label if any, label of root node of the argument spine. In Figure 2, if take *stabilize* as predicate, and *Street* as argument, the two variants are *XP-NNP-street* and *XP-ORGANIZATION*[2] respectively.

PP content word of argument e-tree if the root label of the argument e-tree is PP, anchor of the last daughter node. NE variant of this feature: replace its POS with the NE label if any.

Features from the spine node (SP1) spine node is the landing site between predicate e-tree and argument e-tree. Features include the index along the host spine[3], label of the node, operation involved (*att* or *adj*).

Relative position of predicate and argument in the sentence: before/after.

Order of current child node among its siblings. In pattern 1, predicate e-tree is parent, and argument e-tree is child. This feature refers to the order of argument e-tree among its siblings nodes (with predicate e-tree as parent).

Distance of predicate e-tree and argument tree in the LTAG derivation tree: For example, for pattern 1 and 2, the distance has value 0; for pattern 3, the distance has value 1.

Pattern ID valued 1-7. (see Table 1 and Table 2)

Combination of position and pattern ID, combination of distance and pattern ID, combination of

[2]XP-NNP is a normalized e-tree form used in (Shen et al., 2008) for efficiency and to avoid the problem of sparse data over too many e-trees.

[3]it can either be predicate e-tree or argument e-tree. For example, for pattern P←A, the A(rgument) e-tree is the host spine.

position and order.

Features from intermediate predicate e-tree same features as predicate e-tree features.

Features from spine node of intermediate predicate e-tree and argument e-tree (SP2) for predicate-argument pairs of pattern 3-7. These features are similar to the SP1 features but instead between intermediate predicate e-tree and argument e-tree.

Relative position between predicate e-tree and intermediate e-tree.

Combination relative positions of argument e-tree and intermediate predicate e-tree + relative position of argument e-tree and predicate e-tree.

The features listed above are used to represent each candidate constituent (or node) in the LTAG-spinal derivation tree in training and test data. In both cases, we identify SRLs for nodes for each predicate. In training each node comes with the appropriate semantic role label, or NULL if it does not have any (for the predicate). In test data, we first identify nodes as arguments using these features (ARG v.s. NULL classification) and then classify a node identified as an argument with the particular SRL using one-vs-all binary classification.

4 Experiments

4.1 Data Set

Following the usual convention for parsing and SRL experiments, LTAG-spinal Treebank Section 2-21 is used for training and Section 23 for testing. Propbank argument set is used which includes numbered arguments A0 to A5 and 13 adjunct-like arguments. 454 sentences in the Penn Treebank are skipped from the LTAG-spinal Treebank (Shen et al., 2008)[4], which results in 115 predicate-argument pairs ignored in the test set.

We applied SVM-light (Joachims, 1999) with default linear kernel to feature vectors. 30% of the training samples are used to fine tune the regularization parameter c and the loss-function cost parameter j for both argument identification and classification. With parameter validation experiments, we set $c = 0.1$ and $j = 1$ for {A0, AM-NEG}, $c = 0.1$, $j = 2$ for {A1, A2, A4, AM-EXT} and $c = 0.1$ and $j = 4$ for the rest.

For comparison, we also built up a standard 3-stage phrase-structure based SRL system, where exactly the same data set[5] is used from 2004 February release of the Propbank. SVM-light with linear kernel is used to train on a standard feature set (Xue and Palmer, 2004). The Charniak and Johnson parser (2006) is used to produce the automatic parses. Note that this phrase-structure based SRL system is state-of-the-art and we have included all the features proposed in the literature that use phrase-structure trees. This system obtains a higher SRL accuracy which can be improved only by using global inference and other ways (such as using multiple parsers) to improve the accuracy on automatic parses.

4.2 Results

We compared our LTAG-spinal based SRL system with phrase-structure based one (see the description in earlier sections), for argument identification and classification. In order to analyze the impact of errors in syntactic parsers, results are presented on both gold-standard trees and automatic parses. Based on the fact that nearly 97% e-trees that correspond to the core arguments[6] belong to pattern 1 and 2, which accounts for the largest portion of argument loss in automatic parses, the classification results are also given for these core arguments. We also compare with the CCG-based SRL presented in (Gildea and Hockenmaier, 2003)[7], which has a similar motivation as this paper, except they use the Combinatory Categorial Grammar formalism and the CCGBank syntactic Treebank which was converted from the Penn Treebank.

Scoring strategy To have a fair evaluation of arguments between the LTAG-spinal dependency parse and the Penn Treebank phrase structure, we report the *root/head-word* based scoring strategy for performance comparison, where a case is counted as positive as long as the root of the argument e-tree is correctly identified in LTAG-spinal and the head word of the argument constituent is correctly identified in phrase structure. In contrast, boundary-

[4] Based on (Shen et al., 2008), the skipped 454 sentences amount to less than 1% of the total sentences. 314 of these 454 sentences have gapping structures. Since PTB does not annotate the trace of deleted predicates, additional manual annotation is required to handle these sentences. For the rest of the 146 sentences, abnormal structures are generated due to tagging errors.

[5] The same 454 sentences are ignored.

[6] A0, A1, A2, A3, A4, A5

[7] Their data includes the 454 sentences. However, the missing 115 predicate-argument pairs account for less than 1% of the total number of predicate-argument pairs in the test data, so even if we award these cases to the CCGBank system the system performance gap still remains.

based scoring is more strict in that the string span of the argument must be correctly identified in identification and classification.

Results from using gold standard trees Table 3 shows the results when gold standard trees are used. We can see that with gold-standard derivations, LTAG-spinal obtains the highest precision on identification and classification; it also achieves a competitive f-score (highest f-score for identification) with the recall upper-bound lower by 2-3% than phrase-structure based SRL. However, the recall gap between the two SRL systems gets larger for classification compared to identification[8], which is due to the low recall that is observed with our LTAG-spinal based SRL based on our current set of features. If compare the difference between the root/head-word based score and the boundary based score in the 3 scenarios, we notice that the difference reflects the discrepancy between the argument boundaries. It is not surprising to see that phrase-structure based one has the best match. However, CCGBank appears to have a large degree of mismatch. In this sense, root/head word based scoring provides fair comparison between LTAG-spinal SRL system and the CCGBank SRL system.

Recent work (Boxwell and White, 2008) changes some structures in the CCGBank to correspond more closely with the Probbank annotations. They also resolve split arguments that occur in Propbank and add these annotations into a revised version of the CCGBank. As a result they show that the *oracle* f-score improves by over 2 points over the (Gildea and Hockenmaier, 2003) oracle results for the numbered arguments only (A0, . . ., A5). It remains an open question whether a full SRL system based on a CCG parser trained on this new version of the CCGBank will be competitive against the LTAG-spinal based and phrase-structure based SRL systems.

Results from using automatic parses Table 4 shows the results when automatic parses are used. With automatic parses, the advantage of LTAG-spinal in the precision scores still exists: giving a higher score in both identification and core argument classification; only 0.5% lower for full argument classification. However, with over 6% difference in upper-bound of recall ($\leq$85.6% from LTAG-spinal; $\sim$91.7% from Charniak's parser), the gap in recall becomes larger: increased to $\sim$10% in automatic parses from $\sim$6% in gold-standard trees.

The identification result is not available for CCG-based SRL. In terms of argument classification, it is significantly outperformed by the LTAG-spinal based SRL. In particular, it can be seen that the LTAG-spinal parser performs much better on argument boundaries than CCG-based one.

One thing worth mentioning is that since neither the LTAG-spinal parser nor Charniak's parser provides trace (empty category) information in their output, no trace information is used for LTAG-spinal based SRL or the phrase-structure based SRL even though it is available in their gold-standard trees.

5 Conclusion and Future Work

With a small feature set, the LTAG-spinal based SRL system described in this paper provides the highest precision in almost all the scenarios, which indicates that the shallow semantic relations, e.g., the predicate-argument relations that are encoded in the LTAG-spinal Treebank are useful for SRL, especially when compared to the phrase structure Penn Treebank. (Shen et al., 2008) achieves an f-score of 91.6% for non-trace SRL identification on the entire Treebank by employing a simple rule-based system, which also suggested this conclusion. In other words, there is a tighter connection between the syntax and semantic role labels in the LTAG-spinal representation.

However, in contrast to the high precision, the recall performance of LTAG-spinal based SRL needs a further improvement, especially for the argument classification task. From SRL perspective, on one hand, this may be due to the pattern-based candidate selection, which upper-bounds the number of predicate-argument pairs that can be recovered for SRL; on the other hand, it suggests that the features for argument classification need to be looked at more carefully, compared to the feature selection for argument identification, especially for A2 and A3 (as indicated by our error analysis on the results on the development set). A possible solution is to customize a different feature set for each argument type during classification, especially for contextual information.

Experiments show that when following the pipelined architecture, the performance of LTAG-based SRL is more severely degraded by the syntactic parser, compared to the SRL using phrase

[8] no NULL examples are involved when training for argument classification.

Identification	gold-standard trees (p/r/f%)		
Scoring	LTAG	phrase	CCG
Root/head-word	**96.0**/92.1/**94.0**	93.0/94.0/93.5	n/a
classification (core)	gold-standard trees (p/r/f%)		
Scoring	LTAG	phrase	CCG
Root/head-word	**90.6**/83.4/86.9	87.2/88.4/87.8	82.4/78.6/80.4
classification (full)	gold-standard trees (p/r/f%)		
Scoring	LTAG	phrase	CCG
Root/head-word	**88.2**/81.7/84.8	86.1/87.1/86.6	76.3/67.8/71.8
Boundary	**87.4**/81.0/84.1	86.0/87.0/86.5	67.5/60.0/63.5

Table 3: Using gold standard trees: comparison of the three SRL systems for argument identification, core and full argument classification

Identification	automatic parses (p/r/f%)		
Scoring	LTAG	phrase	CCG
Root/head-word	**85.8**/80.0/82.8	85.8/87.7/86.7	n/a
classification (core)	automatic parses (p/r/f%)		
Scoring	LTAG	phrase	CCG
Root/head-word	**81.0**/71.5/76.0	80.1/82.8/81.4	76.1/73.5/74.8
classification (full)	automatic parses (p/r/f%)		
Scoring	LTAG	phrase	CCG
Root/head-word	78.0/70.0/73.7	78.5/80.3/79.4	71.0/63.1/66.8
Boundary	72.3/65.0/68.5	73.8/75.5/74.7	55.7/49.5/52.4

Table 4: Using automatic parses: comparison of the three SRL systems for argument identification, core and full argument classification

structure and CCG formalism. Even though the left-to-right statistical parser that was trained and evaluated on the LTAG-spinal Treebank achieves an f-score of 89.3% for dependencies on Section 23 of this treebank (Shen and Joshi, 2005), the SRL that used this output is worse than expected. An oracle test shows that via the same 7 patterns, only 81.6% predicate-argument pairs can be recovered from the automatic parses, which is a big drop from 96.1% when we use the LTAG-spinal Treebank trees. Parser accuracy is high overall, but needs to be more accurate in recovering the dependencies between predicate and argument.

Based on the observation that the low recall occurs not only to the SRL when the automatic parses are used but also when the gold trees are used, we would expect that a thorough error analysis and feature calibrating can give us a better idea in terms of how to increase the recall in both cases.

In on-going work, we also plan to improve the dependency accuracy for predicate and argument dependencies by using the SRL predictions as feedback for the syntactic parser. Our hypothesis is that this approach combined with features that would improve the recall numbers would lead to a highly accurate SRL system.

As a final note, we believe that our effort on using LTAG-spinal for SRL is a valuable exploration of the LTAG-spinal formalism and its Treebank resource. We hope our work will provide useful information on how to better utilize this formalism and the Treebank resource for semantic role labeling.

Acknowledgements

We would like to thank Aravind Joshi and Lucas Champollion for their useful comments and for providing us access to the LTAG-spinal Treebank. We would especially like to thank Libin Shen for providing us with the LTAG-spinal statistical parser for our experiments and for many helpful comments.

References

A. Abeillé and O. Rambow, editors. 2001. *Tree Adjoining Grammars: Formalisms, Linguistic Analysis and Processing*. Center for the Study of Language and Information.

Stephen A. Boxwell and Michael White. 2008. Projecting propbank roles onto the ccgbank. In *LREC-2008*.

X. Carreras and L. Màrquez. 2004. Introduction to the CoNLL-2004 Shared Task. In *CoNLL-2004*.

X. Carreras and L. Màrquez. 2005. Introduction to the CoNLL-2005 Shared Task. In *CoNLL-2005*.

J. Chen and O. Rambow. 2003. Use of deep linguistic features for the recognition and labeling of semantic arguments. In *EMNLP-2003*.

C.J. Fillmore, C. Wooters, and C.F. Baker. 2001. Building a large lexical databank which provides deep semantics. In *PACLIC15-2001*.

D. Gildea and J. Hockenmaier. 2003. Identifying semantic roles using combinatory categorial grammar. In *EMNLP-2003*.

D. Gildea and D. Jurafsky. 2002. Automatic labeling of semantic roles. *Computational Linguistics*, 58(3):245–288.

D. Gildea and M. Palmer. 2002. The necessity of parsing for predicate argument recognition. In *ACL-2002*.

K. Hacioglu. 2004. Semantic role labeling using dependency trees. In *COLING-2004*.

T. Joachims. 1999. Making large-scale svm learning practical. *Advances in Kernel Methods - Support Vector Machines*.

Y. Liu and A. Sarkar. 2007. Experimental evaluation of LTAG-based features for semantic role labeling. In *EMNLP-2007*.

M. Palmer, D. Gildea, and P. Kingsbury. 2005. The proposition bank: An annotated corpus of semantic roles. *Computational Linguistics*, 31(1).

S. Pradhan, W. Ward, K. Hacioglu, , J. H. Martin, and D. Jurafsky. 2004. Shallow Semantic Parsing Using Support Vector Machines. In *HLT-NAACL-2004*.

S. Pradhan, W. Ward, K. Hacioglu, , J. H. Martin, and D. Jurafsky. 2005. Semantic role labeling using different syntactic views. In *ACL-2005*.

Yves Schabes and Stuart M. Shieber. 1994. An alternative conception of tree-adjoining derivation. *Computational Linguistics*, 20(1):91–124.

L. Shen and Aravind Joshi. 2005. Incremental ltag parsing. In *HLT-EMNLP-2005*.

L. Shen and A. Joshi. 2008. Ltag dependency parsing with bidirectional incremental construction. In *EMNLP-2008*.

L. Shen, L. Champollion, and A. Joshi. 2008. Ltag-spinal and the treebank: A new resource for incremental, dependency and semantic parsing. *Language Resources and Evaluation*, 42(1):1–19.

L. Shen. 2006. *Statistical LTAG Parsing*. Ph.D. thesis, University of Pennsylvania.

M. Surdeanu, S. Harabagiu, J. Williams, and P. Aarseth. 2003. Using predicate-argument structures for information extraction. In *ACL-2003*.

M. Surdeanu, R. Johansson, A. Meyers, L. Màrquez, and J. Nivre. 2008. The conll 2008 shared task on joint parsing of syntactic and semantic dependencies. In *CoNLL-2008*.

N. Xue and M. Palmer. 2004. Calibrating features for semantic role labeling. In *EMNLP-2004*.

Developing German Semantics on the basis of Parallel LFG Grammars

Sina Zarrieß
Department of Linguistics
University of Potsdam, Germany
sina@ling.uni-potsdam.de

Abstract

This paper reports on the development of a core semantics for German which was implemented on the basis of an English semantics that converts LFG f-structures to flat meaning representations in a Neo-Davidsonian style. Thanks to the parallel design of the broad-coverage LFG grammars written in the context of the ParGram project (Butt et al., 2002) and the general surface independence of LFG f-structure analyses, the development process was substantially facilitated. We also discuss the overall architecture of the semantic conversion system from a crosslinguistic, theoretical perspective.

1 Introduction

This paper reports on the development of a core semantics for German which was implemented on the basis of an English semantics that converts LFG f-structures to flat meaning representations in a Neo-Davidsonian style. The development strategy relies on the parallel design of the broad-coverage LFG grammars written in the context of the ParGram project (Butt et al., 2002). We will first describe the overall architecture of the semantic conversion system as well as the basic properties of the semantic representation. Section 3 discusses the development strategy and the core semantic phenomena covered by the German semantics. In section 3.4, we will discuss the benefits and the limitations of the presented architecture for crosslingual semantics by means of an example phenomenon, the semantics of clause-embedding verbs. The rest of this introduction will be devoted to the broader theoretical context of this work.

Recently, the state of the art in wide-coverage parsing has made wide-coverage semantic processing come into the reach of research in computational semantics (Bos et al., 2004). This shift from the theoretical conception of semantic formalisms to wide-coverage semantic analysis raises many questions about appropriate meaning representations as well as engineering problems concerning the development and evaluation strategies of semantic processing systems. The general aim of this work is to explore wide-coverage LFG syntax as a backbone for linguistically motivated semantic processing.

Research in the framework of LFG has traditionally adopted a crosslingual perspective on linguistic theory (Bresnan, 2000). In the context of the ParGram project, a number of high quality, broad-coverage grammars for several languages have been produced over the years (Butt et al., 2002; Butt and King, 2007).[1] The project's research methodology particularly focusses on **parallelism** which means that the researchers rely on a common syntactic theory as well as development tools, but which also concerns parallelism on the level of syntactic analyses. As the LFG formalism assumes a two-level syntax that di-

[1] Also see the webpage for a nice project overview: http://www2.parc.com/isl/groups/nltt/pargram/

Proceedings of the 2009 Workshop on Grammar Engineering Across Frameworks, ACL-IJCNLP 2009, pages 10–18,
Suntec, Singapore, 6 August 2009.

vides the analysis into a more language and surface dependent constituent structure and a functional structure which basically represents the surface independent grammatical relations of a sentence, it constitutes a particularly appropriate basis for large-scale, multilingual syntax.

Parallel grammar development bears the practical advantage that the resources developped for a particular language can often easily be ported to related languages. Kim et al. (2003) report that the Korean ParGram grammar was constructed in two months by adapting the Japanese grammar for Korean. Moreover, parallel grammars have a straightforward application in multilingual NLP tasks like machine translation (Frank, 1999).

A general motivation for multilingual, deep grammars are higher-level NLP tasks which involve some kind of semantic or meaning-sensititive processing (Butt and King, 2007). The work presented in this paper shows that parallel grammar development not only facilitates porting of grammars, but substantially facilitates the development of resources and applications that involve such a parallel grammar. We rely on the semantic conversion system presented in (Crouch and King, 2006) to implement a system that derives semantic representations from LFG f-structures for German. Due to the parallelism of syntactic f-structure input, the German core semantics could be implemented within a single month.

2 F-Structure Rewriting as an LFG Semantics

Since the early days of LFG, there has been research on interfacing LFG syntax with various semantic formalisms (Dalrymple, 1999). For the English and Japanese ParGram grammar, a broad-coverage, glue semantic construction has been implemented by (Crouch, 1995; Umemoto, 2006). In contrast to these approaches, the semantic conversion described in (Crouch and King, 2006) is not driven by a specific semantic theory about meaning representation, nor by a theoretically motivated apparatus of meaning construction. Therefore, we will talk about "semantic conversion" instead of "construction" in this paper.

The main idea of the system is to convert the surface-independent, syntactic relations and features encoded in an f-structure to normalized semantic relations. The representation simplifies many phenomena usually discussed in the formal semantic literature (see the next section), but is tailored for use in Question Answering (Bobrow et al., 2007a) or Textual Entailment (Bobrow et al., 2007b) applications.

The semantic conversion was implemented by means of the XLE platform, used for grammar development in the ParGram project. It makes use of the built-in transfer module to convert LFG f-structures to semantic representations. The idea to use transfer rules to model a semantic concstruction has also been pursued by (Spreyer and Frank, 2005) who use the transfer module to model a RMRS semantic construction for the German treebank TIGER .

2.1 The Semantic Representation

As a first example, a simplified f-structure analysis for the following sentence and the corresponding semantic representation are given in figure 1.

(1) In the afternoon, John was seen in the park.

The basic idea of the representation exemplified in figure 1 is to represent the syntactic arguments and adjuncts of the main predicate in terms of semantic roles of the context introduced by the main predicate or some higher semantic operator. Thus, the grammatical roles of the main verb in sentence (1) are semantically normalized such that the subject of the passive becomes a theme and an unspecified agent is introduced, see figure 1. The role of the modifiers are specified in terms of their head preposition. This type of semantic representation is inspired by Neo-Davidsonian event semantics (Parsons, 1990). Other semantic properties of the event introduced by the main verb such as tense or nominal properties such as quantification and cardinality are explicitely encoded as conventionalized predications.

The contexts can be tought of as propositions or possible worlds. They are headed by an operator that can recursively embed further contexts. Context embeddings can be induced by lexical items or syntactic constructions and include the following operators: (i) negation (ii) sentential modifiers (*possibly*) (iii) coordination with *or* (iv) conditionals (v) some subordinating conjunctions (*without*) (vi) clause-embedding verbs (*doubt*).

The representation avoids many formal semantic complexities typically discussed in the literature, for instance the interpretation of quantifiers by encoding them as conventionalized semantic predications. Given this skolemized first-order language, the task of textual entailment can be conceived as matching the hypothesis representation against the semantic representation of the text where higher-order reasonning is approximated by explicit entailment rules (e.g. *all* entails *some*, *past* does not entail *present*), see (Bobrow et al., 2007b) for a presentation of an RTE system based on this semantic representation.

2.2 The Semantic Conversion

The XLE transfer module, which we use for the implementation of the conversion of f-structures to semantic representations, is a term rewrite system that applies an ordered list of rewrite rules to a given f-structure input and yields, depending on the rewrite rules, new f-structures (e.g. translated f-structures) or semantic representations. The technical features of the XLE transfer module are described in (Crouch et al., 2006). An important feature for large-scale development is for instance the mechanism of *packed rewriting* that allows for an efficient representation and processing of ambigous f-structure analyses.

```
+VTYPE(%V, %%), +PASSIVE(%V,+),
OBL-AG(%V, %LogicalSUBJ), PTYPE(%LogicalSUBJ,%%),
OBJ(%LogicalSUBJ,%P)
==> SUBJ(%V, %P), arg(%V,%N,%P).
```

Figure 2: Example rewrite rule for passive normalization

The semantic conversion, as described in (Crouch and King, 2006), is not a priori constrained by a formal apparatus of meaning assembly. The main intuition of the conversion is that the embeddings encoded in the syntactic analysis have to be normalized or reencoded in a way such that they correspond to a semantic embedding. An example rewrite rule which applies to passive f-structure analyses and converts them to an active analysis is given in figure refpassive-fig.

In order to be maintainable and extensible, the set of transfer rules producing the semantic representations are organized in a modular way. The main steps of the semantic conversion are given in the following: (i) Flattening of syntax specific f-structure embeddings that don't correspond to semantic embeddings (ii) Canonicalization of grammatical relations (e.g. depassivization) (iii) Marking of items that induce a semantic embedding (which is not encoded in the f-structure) (iv) Linking of f-structure scopes and context of the semantic representation. (v) Removing of f-structure specific features.

An explicitely modular conception of the transfer procedure also facilitates its porting to other languages. Thus, steps 1 and 2 (and partly 3) may be dependent on the language specific f-structure encoding, while the general steps from 3 and 5 don't have to be changed at all when porting the transfer rules to another language.

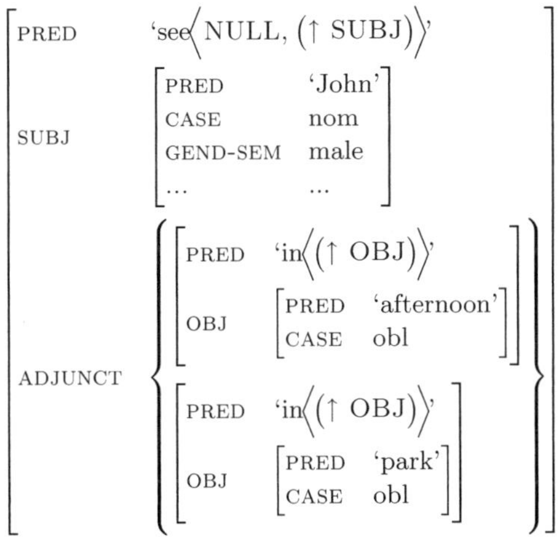


```
ctx_head(t,see),
in_ctx(t, past(see)),
in_ctx(t, cardinality(John,sg)),
in_ctx(t, cardinality(afternoon,sg)),
in_ctx(t, cardinality(park,sg)),
in_ctx(t, specifier(afternoon,the)),
in_ctx(t, specifier(park,the)),
in_ctx(t, time_expr(afternoon:8,+)),
in_ctx(t, proper_name(John,name,John)),
in_ctx(t, role(Agent,see,agent_pro)),
in_ctx(t, role(Theme,see,John)),
in_ctx(t, role(prep(in),see,afternoon)),
in_ctx(t, role(prep(in),see,park))
```

Figure 1: LFG f-structure analysis and corresponding semantic representation

3 From English to German Semantics

3.1 Semantic Grammar Development

In contrast to the various gold standard treebanks available for the development and evaluation of parsers, gold standards for semantic representations are hardly available. This has a number of methodological implications for "semantic grammar" development. For instance, the authors in (de Paiva and King, 2008) argue for large-scale development of a semantics that is based on an application-oriented testsuite of entailment pairs instead of sentences and their theoretically correct representations. However, in the context of this work, we didn't focus on a semantic application, but we wanted to assess the portability of the semantic representations to other languages directly. Adopting such a theory-driven perspective on semantic grammar development, the only possibility to account for the accuracy of the semantic construction is to manually inspect the output of the system for a necessarily small set of input sentences.

Moreover, the transfer scenario complicates the assessment of the system's coverage. While in (Bos et al., 2004), the coverage of the meaning construction can be quantified by the number of syntactic analysis that the construction algorithm can process, the transfer conversion will never fail on a given syntactic input. Since the transfer rules just try to match the input, the unmatched features just pass unchanged to the output and will be probably deleted by some of the catch-all rules which remove remaining syntactic features in the final step of the conversion. Therefore, manual inspection is necessary to see whether the conversion has processed all the input it was supposed to process.

This limited evaluation scenario entails that the semantics developer has to think hard about defining the set of phenomena he wants to cover and document precisely which type of syntactic phenomena his semantics intends to assign an interpretation to. Therefore, in the rest of this section, we will try to give a concrete overview of the type of phenomena that is covered by the English-German semantics.

3.2 A Parallel Testsuite

In consequence to these considerations on evaluation, a central aspect of our development methodology is a testsuite of German sentences which represents the "core semantics" that our systems covers. The multilingual perspective provided a major orientation for the composition of this testsuite. As our base English semantics implicitely defines a set of core phenomena interpreted by the syntax-semantic interface, we dispose of a set of grammatical f-structure relations that receive a particular semantic representation. Fortunately, the developers of the English semantics had documented many "core" transfer rules (assuring the normalization and context embedding) with example phrases or sentences such that one could easily reconstruct the type of phenomenon each transfer rule was intended to analyze.

On the basis of this system documentation, we first conceived an English testsuite where each sentence contained a construction related to the application of a specific transfer rule. For each of the sentences we selected a German sentence which exhibited the German counterpart of the phenomenon targeted in the English sentence. For instance, if a transfer rule for relative clauses fired on a given English sentence we translated the German sentence such that it contained a relative clause. As most of the test sentences target fairly general phenomena at the syntax-semantic interface (see the next section), there was a parallel German realization of the construction in most of the cases.

In cases where no straightforward parallel realization could be found, we recur to a semantically parallel translation. For instance, the English cleft construction exemplified by the following sentence of our testsuite, does not have a syntactically parallel realization in German. In this case, the sentence was translated by a "semantic" equivalent that emphasizes the oblique argument.

(2) a. It is to the store that they went.
b. Zum Markt sind sie gegangen.

During the development process, the testset was further extended. These extensions were due to cases where the English grammar assigns a uniform analysis to some constructions that the German gramamr distinguishes. For instance, while the English grammar encodes oblique arguments the same way it encodes direct objects, the German grammar has a formally slightly different analysis such that rules which fire on obliques in English, don't fire for German input. Now, the final parallel testsuite comprises 200 sentence pairs.

The following enumeration lists the basic morpho-syntactic phenomena covered by our core semantics testsuite.

1. Sentence types (declaratives, interrogatives, quotations etc.)
2. Coordination (of various phrase types)
3. Argument - semantic role mapping, including argument realization normalization (depassivization etc.)
4. Sentential and verbal modification (discursive, propositional, temporal, etc.)
5. Nominal modification (measures, quantifiers, comparatives, etc.)
6. Tense and aspect
7. Appositions and titles
8. Clause-embeddings, relative clauses, gerunds, etc.
9. Predicative and copula constructions
10. Topicalization

It turns out that the abstract conception of LFG f-structure analysis already assumes a major step towards semantic interpretation. Many global syntactic properties are explicitely represented as feature-value pairs, e.g. features for sentence type, mood, tense and aspect. Moreover, the f-structure already contains many information about e.g. the type of nominal phrases (proper names, quantified phrases etc.) or types of modifiers (e.g. adverb types). Finally, this also justifies our testsuite approach since the range of syntactic variation on this abstract level is much smaller than on the level of word-order.

3.3 Parallel Core Semantics

The English core semantics developped by (Crouch and King, 2006) comprises 798 (ordered!) rewrite rules. As we hypothesized that a major part of the English rules will also apply to German f-structure input, we first copied all English transfer rules to the German semantics and then proceeded by manual error correction: For each German test sentence, we manually checked whether the transfer semantics produce an interpretation of the sentence which is parallel to the English analysis. In case a mismatch was detected, the respective rules where changed or added in the German transfer rule set.

To cover the 200 sentences in our parallel testsuite, 47 rewrite rules had to be changed out of the 798 rules which constitute the core English semantics. Out of these 47 rules, 23 rules relate to real structural differences in the f-structure encoding for German and English. The rest of the modifications is mainly due to renamings of the features or lexical items that are hard-coded in the transfer grammar.

While in a more surface-oriented syntax, it would be hardly possible to design largely parallel syntax-semantic interfaces for the range of phenomena listed in the last section, the surface-independence (and the resulting relative crosslingual generality) of LFG f-structures ensures that a major part of the English core semantics straightforward-ly applies to the German input.

An impressive illustration of the language independence of LFG f-structure analyses in the ParGram grammars is the pair of analyses presented in figure 3, produced by the semantic conversion for the example pair in (3).

(3) a. Wo hat Tom gestern geschlafen?
    b. Where did Tom sleep yesterday?

The representation for the German sentence was produced by running the English transfer semantics on German syntactic input. Although the word-order of English and German questions is governed by distinct syntactic principles, the semantic representation of the German sentence is almost entirely correct since the f-structure analyses abstract from the word-order differences. The only fault in the German representation in 3 is the interpretation of the temporal adverb *yesterday* - *gestern*. The transfer rule for temporal verb modification didn't fire because the adverb type features for English and German differ.

3.4 Discussion: Clause-embeddings and Semantic Fine-graininess

The crosslinguistic parallelism of the semantics presented in this paper is also due to the relative coarse-grained level of representation that interprets many phenomena prone to subtle crosslingual divergences (e.g. the interpretation of quantifiers or tense and aspect) in terms of conventionalized predications, e.g. the interpretation of tense as `past(see)` in figure 1. Thus, the real semantic interpretation of these phenomena is deferred to later representation or processing layers, as in this framework, to the definition of entailment relations (Bobrow et al., 2007b). A meaning representation that defers much of the semantic interpretation to the formulation of entailment rules runs the obvious risk of making to few theoretical generalizations which results in very complex entailment rules. This section will briefly illustrate this problem by discussing the representation of clause-embeddings in our semantics.

The various semantic operators defined by the semantic conversion to induce an embedding (see section 2.1) embed a semantic entity of the type `context` which can be roughly considered as the common semantic type of "proposition". An example for the semantic representation of a clause-embedding verb is given in figure 4.

For many semantic applications, such embedded contexts are of particular interest since they often express propositions to

```
ctx_head(ctx(s),schlafen),
ctx_index(t,schlafen),                          ctx_head(ctx(s),sleep),
in_ctx(t,interrogative(ctx(s))),
in_ctx(ctx(s),perf(schlafen)),
in_ctx(ctx(s),pres(schlafen)),
in_ctx(ctx(s),query_term(wo)),
in_ctx(ctx(s),cardinality('Tom',sg)),
in_ctx(ctx(s),proper_name('Tom',name,'Tom')),
in_ctx(ctx(s),role('Agent',schlafen,'Tom')),
in_ctx(ctx(s),role(adeg,gestern,normal)),
in_ctx(ctx(s),role(adeg,wo,normal)),
in_ctx(ctx(s),role(amod,schlafen,gestern)),
in_ctx(ctx(s),role(amod,schlafen,wo))
```

causes the modality of the complement such that it is not necessarily true, while in sentence (7), the embedded clause is necessarily true due to the perfective aspect of the clause-embedding verb. This aspectual matrix-com-plement relation is however only observable for certain types of modality or clause-embedding verbs and has no clear semantic parallel in other languages that don't have aspectual marking.

For another type of clause-embedding verbs, called epistemic verbs, the recent formal semantics literature discusses many examples where the lexical neutral entailment class is overriden by pragmatic interpretation constraints that cause the embedded complement to be interpreted as true although the embedding operator does not entail the veridicality of its complement (Simons, 2006; von Fintel and Gillies, 2007). As an example, consider the following text - hypothesis pair annotated as a valid entailment in the Pascal RTE 3 set altough the hypothesis clearly refers to an embedded proposition in the given text.

(8) Between March and June, scientific observers say, up to 300,000 seals are killed. In Canada, seal-hunting means jobs, but opponents say it is vicious and endangers the species, also threatened by global warming.

(9) Hunting endangers seal species. FOLLOWS (RTE3 ID:225)

Such examples suggest that entailments concern various aspects of the meaning of a sentence or proposition, thus, not only its veridicality but also its temporal properties, informations about involved agents, space and time. These properties are clearly related to the semantic type of the embedded clause.

Purely lexical entailment rules for clause-em-bedding operators will be very hard to formulate in the light of the complex interaction of the various linguistic parameters. These considerations reveal a general trade-off between a representation that generalizes over many (purely) theoretical and crosslingual subtleties and a representation that does not capture certain generalizations which would lead to a more linguistically informed account of entailment relations. Future work on the semantics presented in this paper will have to take such tensions into account and think about the general goals and applications of the semantic representation.

```
ctx_head(t,glauben),
ctx_head(ctx(kennen),kennen)),
ctx_head(ctx(nicht,nicht),
in_ctx(t,role(sem_comp,glauben,ctx(nicht))),
in_ctx(t,role(sem_subj,glauben,'Andreas')),
in_ctx(ctx(kennen),role(sem_obj,kennen,pro)),
in_ctx(ctx(nicht),role(adeg,nicht,normal)),
in_ctx(ctx(nicht),role(amod,ctx(kennen),nicht)
```

Figure 4: Example representation for context embeddings, sentence (4)

4 Conclusion

This work amply illustrates the positive implications of crosslinguistic, parallely designed resources for large-scale linguistic engineering. Due to the abstract f-structure layer in LFG syntax and its parallel implementation in the ParGram project, further resources that build on f-structure representations can be very easily ported to other languages. Future research will have to investigate to what extent this also applies to more distant languages, like Urdu and English for instance.

The paper also discussed some problematic aspects of the development of a large-scale semantic system. The crosslingual development perspective allowed us to define a set of core semantic phenomena covered by the representation. However, from a formal semantic view point, the simplifying representation obstructs potential crosslingual differences in semantic interpretation. Future research still has to be conducted to develop a more general development and evaluation methodology for the representation of meaning.

References

Nicholas Asher. 1993. *Reference to Abstract Objects in Discourse.* Studies in Linguistics and Philosophy. Kluwer Academic Publishers.

Jon Barwise and John Perry. 1999. *Situations and Attitudes.* CSLI Publications.

Rajesh Bhatt, 2006. *Covert Modality in Non-finite Contexts*, volume 8 of *Interface Explorations*, chapter Ability modals and their actuality entailments. Mouton de Gruyter.

Daniel G. Bobrow, Bob Cheslow, Cleo Condoravdi, Lauri Karttunen, Tracy Holloway King, Rowan Nairn, Valeria de Paiva, Charlotte Price, and Annie Zaenen. 2007a. PARC's Bridge question answering system. In Tracy Holloway King and Emily M. Bender, editors, *Proceedings of the GEAF (Grammar Engineering Across Frameworks) 2007 Workshop*, pages 13–15.

Daniel G. Bobrow, Bob Cheslow, Cleo Condoravdi, Lauri Karttunen, Tracy Holloway King, Rowan Nairn, Valeria de Paiva, Charlotte Price, and Annie Zaenen. 2007b. Precision-focused textual inference. In *ACL-PASCAL Workshop on Textual Entailment and Paraphrasing*, pages 28 – 29.

Johan Bos, Stephen Clark, Mark Steedman, James R. Curran, and Julia Hockenmaier. 2004. Wide-coverage semantic representations from a CCG parser. In *COLING '04: Proceedings of the 20th international conference on Computational Linguistics*, page 1240, Morristown, NJ, USA. Association for Computational Linguistics.

Joan Bresnan. 2000. *Lexical-Functional Syntax.* Blackwell, Oxford.

Miriam Butt and Tracy Holloway King. 2007. XLE and XFR: A Grammar Development Platform with a Parser/Generator and Rewrite System. In *International Conference on Natural Language Processing (ICON) Tutorial.*

Miriam Butt, Helge Dyvik, Tracy Holloway King, Hiroshi Masuichi, and Christian Rohrer. 2002. The Parallel Grammar Project.

Richard Crouch and Tracy Holloway King. 2006. Semantics via F-Structure Rewriting. In Miriam Butt and Tracy Holloway King, editors, *Proceedings of the LFG06 Conference.*

Dick Crouch, Mary Dalrymple, Tracy King, John Maxwell, and Paula Newman, 2006. *XLE Documentation.*

Dick Crouch. 1995. Packed Rewriting for Mapping Semantics to KR. In *Proceedings of the International Workshop on Computational Semantics.*

Mary Dalrymple. 1999. *Semantics and Syntax in Lexical Functional Grammar: The Resource Logic Approach.* MIT Press, Cambridge, Mass.

Valeria de Paiva and Tracy Holloway King. 2008. Designing testsuites for grammar-based systems in applications. In *Proc. of the COLING GEAF Workshop 2008.*

Anette Frank. 1999. From Parallel Grammar Development towards Machine Translation (shortened version). In Miriam Butt and Tracy Holloway King, editors, *Proceedings of the LFG-99 Conference*, CSLI Online Publications, University of Manchester. Section 4 of: Miriam Butt and Stefanie Dipper and Anette Frank and Tracy Holloway King.

Talmy Givon. 1990. *Syntax*, volume 2. Benjamins.

Roger Kim, Mary Dalrymple, Ronald M. Kaplan, Tracy Holloway King, Hiroshi Masuichi, and Tomoko Ohkuma. 2003. Multilingual Grammar Development via Grammar Porting. . In *ESSLLI 2003 Workshop on Ideas and Strategies for Multilingual Grammar Development.*

Rowan Nairn, Cleo Condoravdi, and Lauri Karttunen. 2006. Computing relative polarity for textual inference. In *Inference in Computational Semantics (ICoS-5).*

Terence Parsons. 1990. *Events in the semantics of English*, volume 19 of *Current studies in linguistics series ; 19.* MIT Pr., Cambridge, Mass. [u.a.].

Mandy Simons. 2006. Observations on embedding verbs, evidentiality, and presupposition. *Lingua.*

Kathrin Spreyer and Anette Frank. 2005. The TIGER 700 RMRS Bank: RMRS Construction from Dependencies. In *Proceedings of LINC 2005*, pages 1–10.

Hiroshi Umemoto. 2006. Implementing a Japanese Semantic Parser Based on Glue Approach. In *Proceedings of The 20th Pacific Asia Conference on Language, Information and Computation.*

Kai von Fintel and Anthony S. Gillies. 2007. An opinionated guide to epistemic modality. In Tamar Gendler Szabo and John Hawthorne, editors, *Oxford Studies in Epistomology, Vol. 2.* Oxford University Press.

Mining of Parsed Data to Derive Deverbal Argument Structure

Olga Gurevich **Scott A. Waterman**
Microsoft / Powerset
475 Brannan Street, Ste. 330
San Francisco, CA 94107
{olya.gurevich, scott.waterman}@microsoft.com

Abstract

The availability of large parsed corpora and improved computing resources now make it possible to extract vast amounts of lexical data. We describe the process of extracting structured data and several methods of deriving argument structure mappings for deverbal nouns that significantly improves upon non-lexicalized rule-based methods. For a typical model, the F-measure of performance improves from a baseline of about 0.72 to 0.81.

1 Introduction

There is a long-standing division in natural language processing between symbolic, rule-based approaches and data-driven, statistical ones. Rule-based, human-curated approaches are thought to be more accurate for linguistic constructions explicitly covered by the rules. However, such approaches often have trouble scaling up to a wider range of phenomena or different genres of text. There have been repeated moves towards hybridized approaches, in which rules created with human linguistic intuitions are supplemented by automatically derived corpus data (cf. (Klavans and Resnik, 1996)).

Unstructured corpus data for English can easily be found on the Internet. Large corpora of text annotated with part of speech information are also available (such as the British National Corpus). However, it is much harder to find widely available, large corpora annotated for syntactic or semantic structure. The Penn Treebank (Marcus et al., 1993) has until recently been the only such corpus, covering 4.5M words in a single genre of financial reporting. At the same time, the accuracy and speed of syntactic parsers has been improving greatly, so that in recent years it has become possible to automatically create parsed corpora of reasonable quality, using much larger amounts of text with greater genre variation. For many NLP tasks, having more training data greatly improves the quality of the resulting models (Banko and Brill, 2001), even if the training data are not perfect.

We have access to the entire English-language text of Wikipedia (about 2M pages) that was parsed using the XLE parser (Riezler et al., 2002), as well as an architecture for distributed data-mining within this corpus, called Oceanography (Waterman, 2009). Using the parsed corpus, we extract a large volume of dependency relations and derive lexical models that significantly improve a rule-based system for determining the underlying argument structure of deverbal noun constructions.

2 Deverbal Argument Mapping

Deverbal nouns, or nominalizations, are nouns that designate some aspect of the event referred to by the verb from which they are morphologically derived (Quirk et al., 1985). For example, the noun *destruction* refers to the action described by the verb *destroy*, and *destroyer* may refer to the agent of that event. Deverbal nouns are very common in English texts: by one count, about half of all sentences in written text contain at least one deverbal noun (Gurevich et al., 2008). Thus, a computational system that aims to match multiple ways of expressing the same underlying events (such as question answering or search) must be able to deal with deverbal nouns.

To interpret deverbal constructions, one must be able to map nominal and prepositional modifiers to the various roles in the verbal frame. For intransitive verbs, almost any argument of the deverbal noun is mapped to the verb's subject, e.g. *abundance of food* gives rise to *subj(abound, food)*. If the underlying verb is transitive, and the deverbal noun has two arguments, the mappings are also fairly straightforward. For example, the phrase *Carthage's defeat by Rome* gives rise to

Proceedings of the 2009 Workshop on Grammar Engineering Across Frameworks, ACL-IJCNLP 2009, pages 19–27,
Suntec, Singapore, 6 August 2009.

the arguments *subj(defeat, Rome)* and *obj(defeat, Carthage)*, based on knowledge that a "by" argument usually maps to the subject, and the possessive in the presence of a "by" argument usually maps to the object (Nunes, 1993).

However, in many cases a deverbal noun has only one argument, even though the underlying verb may be transitive. In such cases, our system has to decide whether to map the lone argument of the deverbal onto the subject or object of the verb. This mapping is in many cases obvious to a human: e.g., *the king's abdication* corresponds to *subj(abdicate, king)*, whereas *the room's adornment* corresponds to *obj(adorn, room)*. In some cases, the mapping is truly ambiguous, e.g., *They enjoyed the support of the Queen* vs. *They jumped to the support of the Queen*. Yet in other cases, the lone argument of the deverbal noun is neither the subject nor the object of the underlying verb, but it may correspond to a different (e.g. prepositional) argument of the verb, as in *the travels of 1996* (corresponding to *someone traveled in 1996*). Finally, in some cases the deverbal noun is being used in a truly nominal sense, without an underlying mapping to a verb, as in *Bill Gates' foundation*, and the possessive is not a verbal argument.

The predictive models in this paper focus on this case of single arguments of deverbal nouns with transitive underlying verbs. To constrain the scope of the task, we focus on possessive arguments, like *the room's adornment*, and 'of' arguments, like *the support of the Queen*. Our goal is to improve the accuracy of verbal roles assigned in such cases by creating lexically-specific preferences for individual deverbal noun / verb pairs. Some of our experiments also take into account some lexical properties of the deverbal noun's arguments. The lexical preferences are derived by comparing argument preferences of verbs with those of related deverbal nouns, derived from a large parsed corpus using Oceanography.

2.1 Current Deverbal Mapping System

We have a list of approximately 4000 deverbal noun / verb pairs, constructed from a combination of WordNet's derivational links (Fellbaum, 1998), NomLex (Macleod et al., 1998), NomLexPlus (Meyers et al., 2004b) and some independent curation. In the current system implementation, we attempt to map deverbal nouns onto corresponding verbs using a small set of heuristics described in (Gurevich et al., 2008). We distinguish between event nouns like *destruction*, agentive nouns like *destroyer*, and patient-like nouns like *employee*.

If a deverbal noun maps onto a transitive verb and has only one argument, the heuristics are as follows. Arguments of agentive nouns become objects while the nouns themselves become subjects, so *the ship's destroyer* maps to *subj(destroy, destroyer); obj(destroy, ship)*. Arguments of patient-like nouns become subjects while the nouns themselves become objects, so *the company's employee* becomes *subj(employ, company); obj(employ, employee)*.

The difficult case of event nouns is currently handled through default mappings: possessive arguments become subjects (e.g., *his confession* $\mapsto$ *subj(confess, he)*), and 'of' arguments become objects (e.g., *confession of sin* $\mapsto$ *obj(confess, sin)*). However, as we have seen from examples above, these defaults are not always correct. The correct mapping depends on the lexical nature of the deverbal noun and its corresponding verb, and possibly on properties of the possessive or 'of' argument as well.

2.2 System Background

The deverbal argument mapping occurs in the context of a larger semantic search application, where the goal is to match alternate forms expressing similar concepts. We are currently processing the entire text of the English-language Wikipedia, consisting of about 2M unique pages.

Parsing in this system is done using the XLE parser (Kaplan and Maxwell, 1995) and a broad-coverage grammar of English (Riezler et al., 2002; Crouch et al., 2009), which produces constituent structures and functional structures in accordance with the theory of Lexical-Functional Grammar (Dalrymple, 2001).

Parsing is followed by a semantic processing phase, producing a more abstract argument structure. Semantic representations are created using the *Transfer* system of successive rewrite rules (Crouch and King, 2006). Numerous constructions are normalized and rewritten (e.g., passives, relative clauses, etc.) to maximize matching between alternate surface forms. This is the step in which deverbal argument mapping occurs.

2.3 Evaluation Data

To evaluate the performance of the current and experimental argument mappings, we extracted a random set of 1000 sentences from the parsed Wikipedia corpus in which a deverbal noun had a single possessive argument. Each sentence was manually annotated with the verb role mapping between the deverbal and the possessive arguments. One of six labels were assigned:

- Subject, e.g. *John's attention*
- Object, e.g. *arrangement of flowers*
- Other: there is an underlying verb, but the relationship between the verb and the argument is neither subject nor object; these relations often appear as prepositional arguments in the verbal form, e.g. *Declaration of Delhi*
- Noun modifier: the argument modifies the nominal sense of the deverbal noun, rather than the underlying verb, although there is still an underlying event, as in *director of 25 years*
- Not deverbal: the deverbal noun is not used to designate an event in this context, e.g. *the rest of them*
- Error: the parser incorrectly identified the argument as modifying the deverbal, or as being the only argument of the deverbal

Similarly, we extracted a sample of 750 sentences in which a deverbal noun had a single 'of' argument, and annotated those manually.

The distribution of annotations is summarized in Table 1. For possessive arguments, the prevalent role was subject, and for 'of' arguments it was object.

The defaults will correctly assign the majority of arguments roles.

	Possessive	'Of'
total	1000	750
unique deverbals	423	338
subj	**511 (51%)**	158 (21%)
obj	335 (34%)	**411 (55%)**
other	28 (3%)	50 (7%)
noun mod	23 (2%)	18 (2%)
not deverbal	21 (2%)	40 (5%)
error	82 (8%)	73 (10%)

Table 1: Evaluation Role Judgements, with defaults in **bold**

2.4 Lexicalizing Role Mappings

Our basic premise is that knowledge about role-mapping behavior of particular verbs will inform the role-mapping behavior of their corresponding deverbal nouns. For example, if a particular argument of a given verb surfaces as the verb's subject more often than as object, we might also prefer the subject role when the same argument occurs as a modifier of the corresponding deverbal noun. However, as nominal modification constructions impose their own role-mapping preferences (e.g., possessives are more likely to be subjects than objects), we expect different distributions of arguments to appear in the various deverbal modification patterns. Making use of this intuition requires collecting sufficient information about corresponding arguments of verbs and deverbal nouns. This is available, given a large parsed corpus, a reasonably accurate and fast parser, and enough computing capacity. The remainder of the paper details our data extraction, model-building methods, and the results of some experiments.

3 Data Collection

Oceanography is a pattern extraction and statistics language for analyzing structural relationships in corpora parsed using XLE (Waterman, 2009). It simplifies the task of programming for NL analysis over large corpora, and the sorting, counting, and distributional analysis that often characterizes statistical NLP. This corpus processing language is accompanied by a distributed runtime, which uses cluster computing to match patterns and collect statistics simultaneously across many machines. This is implemented in a specialized distributed framework for parsing and text analysis built on top of Hadoop (D. Cutting et al.,). Oceanography programs compile down to distributed programs which run in this cluster environment, allowing the NL researcher to state declaratively the data gathering and analysis tasks.

A typical program consists of two declarative parts, a *pattern matching* specification, and a set of *statistics* declarations. The pattern matching section is written using *Transfer*, a specialized language for identifying subgraphs in the dependency structures used in XLE (Crouch and King, 2006). Transfer rules use a declarative syntax for specifying elements and their relations; in this way, it is much like a very specialized *awk* or *grep* for matching within parse trees and dependency graphs.

Statistics over these matched structures are

also stated declaratively. The researcher states which sub-elements or tuples are to be counted, and the resulting compiled program will output counts. Conditional distributions and comparisons between distributions are available as well.

3.1 Training Data

Using Oceanography, we extracted two sets of relations from the parsed Wikipedia corpus, *FullWiki*, with approximately 2 million documents. A smaller 10,000-document subset, the *10K* set, was used in initial experiments. Some comparative results are shown to indicate effects of corpus size on results. Summary corpus statistics are shown in table 2. The two sets were:

1. All verb-argument pairs, using verb and argument lemmas. We recorded the verb, the argument, the kind of relation between them (e.g., subject, object, etc.), and part of speech of the argument, distinguishing also among pronouns, names, and common nouns. For each combination, we record its frequency of occurrence.

2. All deverbal-argument pairs, using deverbal noun and argument lemmas. We recorded the deverbal noun, the argument, the kind of relation (e.g., possessive, 'of', prenominal modifier, etc.) and part of speech of the argument. We record the frequency of occurrence for each combination.

Some summary statistics about the extracted data are in Table 2.

FullWiki training data	
Documents	2 million
Sentences	121,428,873
Deverbal nouns with arguments	4,596
Unique verbs with deverbals	3,280
Verbs with arguments	7,682
Deverbal - role - argument sets	21,924,405
Deverbal - argument pairs	12,773,621
Deverbals with any poss argument	3,802
Possessive deverbal - argument pairs	611,192
Most frequent: *poss(work, he)*	75,343
Deverbals with any 'of' argument	4,075
'Of' deverbal- argument pairs	2,108,082
Most frequent: *of(end, season)*	15,282
Verb - role - argument sets	72,150,246
Verb - argument pairs	40,895,810
Overlapping pairs	5,069,479
Deverbals with overlapping arguments	3,211

Table 2: Training Data

4 Assigning Roles

The present method is based on projecting argument type preferences from the verbal usage to the deverbal. The intuition is that if an argument X is preferred as the subject (object) of verb V, then it will also be preferred in the semantic frame of an occurrence (N, X) with the corresponding deverbal noun N.

We model these preferences directly using the relative frequency of subject and object occurrences of each possible argument with each verb. Even with an extremely large corpus, it is unlikely that one will find direct evidence for all such combinations, and one will need to generalize the prediction.

4.1 Deverbal-only Model

The first model, *all-arg*, specializes only for the deverbal, and generalizes over all arguments, relying on the overall preference of subject v. object for the set of arguments that appear with both verb and deverbal forms. Take as an example deverbal nouns with possessive arguments (e.g., *the city's destruction*). Given the phrase (X's N), where N is a deverbal noun related to verb V, F_d(N, V, X) is a function that assigns one of the roles $subj, obj, unknown$ to the pair (V, X). In this deverbal only model, the function depends on N and V only, and not on the argument X. F_d for a any pair (N, V) is calculated as follows:

1. Find all arguments X that occur in the construction "N's X" as well as either *subj(V, X)* or *obj(V, X)*. X, N, and V have all been lemmatized. For example, *poss(city, destruction)* occurs 10 times in the corpus; *subj(destroy, city)* occurs 3 times, and *obj(destroy, city)* occurs 12 times. This approach conflates instances of *the city's destruction*, *the cities' destruction*, *the city's destructions*, etc.

2. For each argument X, calculate the ratio between the number of occurrences of *subj(V, X)* and *obj(V, X)*. If the argument occurs as subject more than 1.5 times as often as the object, increment the count of subject-preferring arguments of N by 1. If the argument occurs as object more than 1.5 times as often as subject (as would be the case with *(destroy, city)*), increment the count of object-preferring arguments. If the ratio in frequencies of occurrence is less than the cutoff ratio

of 1.5, neither count is incremented. In addition to the number of arguments with each preference, we keep track of the total number of instances for each argument preference, summed up over all individual arguments with that preference.

3. Compare the number of subject-preferring arguments of N with the number of object-preferring arguments. If one is greater than the other by more than 1.5 times, state that the deverbal noun N has a preference for mapping its possessive arguments to the appropriate verbal role. We ignore cases where the total number of occurrences of the winning arguments is too small to be informative (in the current model, we require it to be greater than 1).

If there is insufficient evidence for a deverbal N, we fall back to the default preference across all deverbals. Subject and object co-occurrences with the verb forms are always counted, regardless of other arguments the verb may have in each sentence, on the intuition that the semantic role preference of the argument is relatively unaffected and that this will map to the deverbal construction even when the possessive is the only argument. Summary preferences for *all-args* are shown in Table 3.

The same algorithm was applied to detect argument preferences for deverbals with 'of' arguments (such as *destruction of the city*). Summary preferences are shown in Table 4.

4.2 Deverbal + Argument Animacy Model

The second model tries to capture the intuition that animate arguments often behave differently than inanimate ones: in particular, animate arguments are more often agents, encoded syntactically as subjects.

We calculated argument preferences separately for two classes of arguments: (1) animate pronouns such as *he*, *she*, *I*; and (2) nouns that were not identified as names by our name tagger. We assumed that arguments in the first group were animate, whereas arguments in the second group were not. In these experiments, we did not try to classify named entities as animate or inanimate, resulting in less training data for both classes of arguments. This strategy also incorrectly classifies common nouns that refer to people (e.g., occupation names such as *teacher*).

The results of running both models on the 10K and FullWiki training sets are in Table 3 for possessive arguments and Table 4 for 'of' arguments.

For possessives, animate arguments preferred subject role mappings much more than the average across all arguments. Inanimate arguments also on the whole preferred subject mappings, but much less strongly.

For 'of' arguments, in most cases there were more object-preferring verbs, except for verbs with animate arguments, which overwhelmingly preferred subjects. We might therefore expect there to be a difference in performance between the model that treats all arguments equally and the model that takes argument animacy into account.

Model: *all-arg*		
	10K	FullWiki
Subj-preferring	**391 (65%)**	**1786 (67%)**
Obj-preferring	207 (35%)	884 (33%)
Total	598 (100%)	2670 (100%)
Model: *animacy*		
Subj-pref animate	**370 (78%)**	**1941 (79%)**
Obj-pref animate	106 (22%)	511 (21%)
Total animate	476 (100%)	2452 (100%)
Subj-pref inanimate	45 (47%)	**990 (57%)**
Obj-pref inanimate	**51 (53%)**	748 (43%)
Total inanimate	96 (100%)	1738 (100%)

Table 3: Possessive argument preferences

Model: *all-arg*		
	10K	FullWiki
Subj-preferring	143 (30%)	839 (29%)
Obj-preferring	**328 (70%)**	**2036 (71%)**
Total	471 (100%)	2875 (100%)
Model: *animacy*		
Subj-pref animate	**70 (83%)**	**1196 (74%)**
Obj-pref animate	14 (17%)	423 (26%)
Total animate	84 (100 %)	1619 (100%)
Subj-pref inanimate	83 (23%)	699 (25%)
Obj-pref inanimate	**272 (77%)**	**2068 (75%)**
Total inanimate	355 (100%)	2767 (100%)

Table 4: 'Of' argument preferences

5 Experiments

The base system against which we compare these models uses the output of the parser, identifies deverbal nouns and their arguments, and applies the heuristics described in Section 2.1 to obtain verb roles. Recall that possessive arguments of transitive deverbals map to the subject role, and 'of' arguments map to object. Also recall that these rules apply only to eventive deverbals; mapping rules for known agentive and patient-like deverbals remain as before.

In the evaluation, the experimental models take precedence: if the model predicts an outcome, it is used. The default system behavior is used as a fallback when the model does not have sufficient evidence to make a prediction. This *stacking* of models allows the use of corpus evidence when available, and generalized defaults otherwise.

For the *animacy* model, we used our full system to detect whether the argument of a deverbal was animate (more precisely, human). In addition to the animate pronouns used to generate the model, we also considered person names, as well as common nouns that had the hypernym 'person' in WordNet. If the argument was animate and the model had a prediction, that was used. If no prediction was available for animate arguments, then the inanimate prediction was used. Failing that, the prediction falls back to the general defaults.

5.1 Possessive Arguments of Deverbal Nouns

Model predictions were compared against the hand-annotated evaluation set described in Section 2.3. For each sentence in the evaluation set, we used the models to make a two-way prediction with respect to the default mapping: is the possessive argument of the deverbal noun an underlying subject or not. We ignored test sentences marked as having erroneous parses, leaving 918 (of 1000 annotated). Since we were evaluating the accuracy of the 'subject' label, all non-subject roles (object, "other", "not a deverbal", and "nominal modifier") were in the same class. The baseline for comparison is the default 'subject' role.

The possible outcomes for each sentence were:

- True Positive: Expected role and role produced by the system are "subject"
- True Negative: Expected role is not subject, and the model did not produce the label subject. Expected role and produced role may differ (e.g. expected role may be "other", and the model may produce "object", but since neither one is "subject", this counts as correct
- False Positive: Expected role is not subject, but the model produced subject
- False Negative: Expected role is subject, but the model produced some other role

As a quick evaluation, we compared baseline and model-predicted results directly in the *surface string* of the sentences, without reparsing the sentences or using the semantic rewrite rules. The advantage of this evaluation is that it is very fast to run and is easily reproducible outside of our specialized environment. This evaluation differed from the full-pipeline evaluation in two ways: (1) it did not distinguish event deverbals from agentive and patient-like deverbals, thus possibly introducing errors, and (2) it did not look up all argument lemmas to find out their animacy. This baseline had precision of 0.56; recall of 1.0, and an F-measure of 0.72.

The complete evaluation uses our full NL pipeline, reparsing the sentences and applying all of our deverbal mapping rules as described above. The baseline for this evaluation had a precision of 0.65, recall of 0.94, and F-measure of 0.77. The differences in the two baselines are mostly due to the full-pipeline evaluation having different mapping rules for agentive and patient-like deverbals.

5.1.1 Results

Results of applying the models are summarized in Table 5, for all models, trained with both the smaller and the larger data sets, and measured with and without using the full pipeline.

All models performed better than the baseline. The *all-arg* model did about the same as the *animacy* model with both training sets. We suggest some reasons for this in the next section.

It is unambiguously clear that adding lexical knowledge to the rule system, even when this knowledge is derived from a relatively small training set, significantly improves performance, and also that more training data leads to greater improvements.

Model	Training	Precision	Recall	F-measure
		Surface String Measure		
Baseline	-	0.56	1.00	0.72
all-arg	10K	0.64	0.92	0.76
animacy	10K	0.62	0.93	0.75
all-arg	**FullWiki**	**0.68**	**0.95**	**0.81**
animacy	FullWiki	0.70	0.92	0.79
		Full NL pipeline		
Baseline	-	0.65	0.94	0.77
all-arg	10K	0.75	0.88	0.81
animacy	10K	0.73	0.90	0.80
all-arg	**FullWiki**	**0.78**	**0.90**	**0.84**
animacy	FullWiki	0.81	0.88	0.84

Table 5: Performance on deverbal nouns with one possessive argument

5.1.2 Error Analysis and Discussion

We looked at the errors produced by the best-performing model, *all-arg* trained on the FullWiki set. There were 49 false negatives (i.e. cases where the human judge decided that the underlying relationship between the deverbal and its argument is 'subject', but our system produced a different relation or no relation at all), covering 39 unique deverbal nouns. Of these, 20 deverbal nouns were predicted by the model to prefer objects (e.g., *Hopkins' accusation*), and 19 did not get assigned either subject or object due to other errors (including a few mislabeled evaluation sentences).

Some of the false negatives involved deverbal nouns that refer to reciprocal predicates such as *his marriage*, or causative ones such as *Berlin's unity*, which could map to subject or objects. Our current system does not allow us to express such ambiguity, but it is a possible future improvement.

Looking at the false negatives produced by the *all-arg* model, 3 deverbal nouns received more accurate predictions with the *animacy* model (e.g., *his sight*; *Peter Kay's statement*). Intuitively, the *animacy* model should in general make more informed decisions about the argument mappings because it takes properties of individual arguments into account. However, as we have seen, it does not in fact outperform the model that treats all arguments the same way.

We believe this is due to the fact that the animacy model was trained on less data than the *all-arg* model, because we only considered animate pronouns and common nouns when generating argument-mapping predictions. Excluding all named entities and non-animate pronouns most likely had an effect on the number of deverbals for which the model was able to make accurate predictions. In the next iteration, we would like to use all available arguments, relying on the named entity type and information available in WordNet for common nouns to distinguish between animate and inanimate arguments.

The *all-arg* model evaluation resulted in 131 false positives (cases where the model predicted the relation to be 'subject', but the human judge thought it was something else). Of these, 105 were marked by the human judge as having objects, 8 as having a verbal relation other than subject or object, 9 as having nominal modifiers, 9 has having no deverbal.

Altogether, false positives covered 85 unique verbs. Of these, 48 had been explicitly predicted by our model to prefer subjects, and the rest had no explicit prediction, thus defaulting to having a subject. 3 of these deverbals would have been correctly identified as having objects by the *animacy* model (e.g., *his composition*; *her representation*).

Although it is hard to predict the outcome of a statistical model, we feel that more reliable information about the animacy of arguments at training time would improve the performance of the *animacy* model, potentially making it better than the *all-arg* model.

5.2 'Of' Arguments of Deverbal Nouns

The evaluation procedure for 'of' arguments was the same as for possessive arguments, except that the default argument mapping was 'object', and the evaluated decision was whether a particular role was object or non-object. Ignoring sentence with erroneous parses, we had 677 evaluation examples.

5.2.1 Results

Results for all models are summarized in Table 6. All models outperformed the baseline on all training sets and on both the surface or full-pipeline measures.

As with possessive arguments, the *all-arg* and *animacy* models performed about the same, with both the FullWiki and 10K training sets.

The 10K-trained *animacy* model did not do as poorly as might have been expected given its low prediction rate for deverbals with animate arguments in our evaluation set. The better-than-expected performance may be explained by low incidence of animate arguments in this set.

Model	Training	Precision	Recall	F-measure
Surface String Measure				
Baseline	-	0.60	1.00	0.75
all-arg	10K	0.68	0.97	0.80
animacy	10K	0.66	0.94	0.78
all-arg	**FullWiki**	**0.71**	**0.97**	**0.82**
animacy	FullWiki	0.70	0.91	0.79
Full NL pipeline				
Baseline	-	0.61	0.89	0.73
all-arg	10K	0.71	0.86	0.78
animacy	10K	0.70	0.85	0.77
all-arg	**FullWiki**	**0.78**	**0.87**	**0.82**
animacy	FullWiki	0.80	0.85	0.82

Table 6: Performance on deverbal nouns with one 'of' argument

5.2.2 Error Analysis and Discussion

We looked at the errors produced by the best-performing model, *all-arg* trained on the FullWiki set. There were 53 false negatives (cases where the human judged marked the relation as 'object' but the system marked it as something else), covering 42 unique deverbal nouns. Of these 7 were (incorrectly) predicted by the model to prefer subjects (e.g., *operation of a railway engine*), and the rest were misidentified due to other errors.

There were 101 false positives (cases where the system marked the role as object, but the human judge disagreed). Of these, the human judged marked 54 as subject, 21 as other verbal role, 13 as nominal modifier, and 13 as non-deverbal.

Of the 72 unique deverbals in the false-positive set, our model incorrectly predicted that 38 should prefer objects (such as *Adoration of the Magi*; *under the direction of Bishop Smith*)). For 30 deverbals, the model made no prediction, and the default mapping to object turned out to be incorrect. It is unclear to what extent better information about animacy would have helped.

6 Related Work

One of the earliest computational attempts to derive argument structures for deverbal nouns is (Hull and Gomez, 1996), with hand-crafted mapping rules for a small set of individual nouns, exemplifying a highly precise but not easily scalable method.

In recent years, NomBank (Meyers et al., 2004a) has provided a set of about 200,000 manually annotated instances of nominalizations with arguments, giving rise to supervised machine-learned approaches such as (Pradhan et al., 2004) and (Liu and Ng, 2007), which perform fairly well in the overall task of classifying deverbal arguments. However, no evaluation results are provided for specific, problematic classes of nominal arguments such as possessives; it is likely that the amount of annotations in NomBank is insufficient to reliably map such cases onto verbal arguments.

(Padó et al., 2008) describe an unsupervised approach that, like ours, uses verbal argument patterns to deduce deverbal patterns, though the resulting labels are semantic roles used in SLR tasks (cf. (Gildea and Jurafsky, 2000)) rather than syntactic roles. A combination of our much larger training set and the sophisticated probabilistic methods used by Padó et al. would most likely improve performance for both syntactic and semantic roles labelling tasks.

7 Conclusions and Future Work

We have demonstrated that large amounts of lexical data derived from an unsupervised parsed corpus improve role assignment for deverbal nouns. The improvements are significant even with a relatively small training set, relying on parses that have not been hand-corrected, using a very simple prediction model. Larger amounts of extracted data improve performance even more.

There is clearly still headroom for improvement in this method. In a pilot study, we used argument preferences for individual deverbal-argument pairs, falling back to deverbal-only generalizations when more specific patterns were not available. This model had slightly higher precision and slightly lower recall than the deverbal-only model, suggesting that a more sophisticcated probabilistic prediction model may be needed.

In addition, performance should improve if we allow non-binary decisions: in addition to mapping deverbal arguments to subject or object of the underlying verb, we could allow mappings such as "unknown" or "ambiguous". The same training sets can be used to produce a model that makes a 3- or 4-way split. In the possessive and 'of' sets, the "unknown / ambiguous" class would cover between 15% and 20% of all the data. This third possibility becomes even more important for other deverbal arguments. For example, if the deverbal noun has a prenominal modifier (as in *city destruction*), in a third of the cases the underlying relation is neither the subject nor the object (Lapata, 2002).

And, of course, the methodology of extracting lexical preferences based on large parsed corpora can be applied to many other NL tasks not related to deverbal nouns.

Acknowledgments

We gratefully acknowledge the helpful advice and comments of our colleagues Tracy Holloway King and Dick Crouch, as well as the three anonymous reviewers.

References

Michele Banko and Eric Brill. 2001. Scaling to very very large corpora for natural language disambiguation. In *ACL*, pages 26–33.

Richard S. Crouch and Tracy Holloway King. 2006. Semantics via f-structure rewriting. In *Proceedings of the Lexical Functional Grammar Conference 2006*.

Dick Crouch, Mary Dalrymple, Ron Kaplan, Tracy Holloway King, John Maxwell, and Paula Newman. 2009. XLE Documentation. Available On-line.

D. Cutting et al. Apache Hadoop Project. http://hadoop.apache.org/.

Mary Dalrymple. 2001. *Lexical Functional Grammar*. Academic Press. Syntax and Semantics, volume 34.

Christiane Fellbaum, editor. 1998. *WordNet: An Electronic Lexical Database*. The MIT Press.

Daniel Gildea and Daniel Jurafsky. 2000. Automatic labeling of semantic roles. In *Proceedings of the 38th Annual Meeting of the Association for Computational Linguistics*, pages 512–520, Hong Kong, October. Association for Computational Linguistics.

Olga Gurevich, Richard Crouch, Tracy Holloway King, and Valeria de Paiva. 2008. Deverbal nouns in knowledge representation. *Journal of Logic and Computation*, 18:385–404.

Richard D. Hull and Fernando Gomez. 1996. Semantic interpretation of nominalizations. In *AAAI/IAAI, Vol. 2*, pages 1062–1068.

Ronald Kaplan and John T. Maxwell. 1995. A method for disjunctive constraint satisfaction. In *Formal Issues in Lexical-Functional Grammar*. CSLI Press.

Judith Klavans and Philip Resnik, editors. 1996. *The Balancing Act. Combining Symbolic and Statistical Approaches to Language*. The MIT Press.

Maria Lapata. 2002. The disambiguation of nominalizations. *Computational Linguistics*, 28(3):357–388.

Chang Liu and Hwee Tou Ng. 2007. Learning predictive structures for semantic role labeling of nombank. In *ACL*.

Catherine Macleod, Ralph Grishman, Adam Meyers, Leslie Barrett, and Ruth Reeves. 1998. NOMLEX: A lexicon of nominalizations. In *Proceedings of EURALEX'98*.

Mitchell P. Marcus, Beatrice Santorini, and Mary Ann Marcinkiewicz. 1993. Building a large annotated corpus of english: The penn treebank. *Computational Linguistics*, 19(2):313–330.

A. Meyers, R. Reeves, C. Macleod, R. Szekely, V. Zielinska, B. Young, and R. Grishman. 2004a. The nombank project: An interim report. In A. Meyers, editor, *HLT-NAACL 2004 Workshop: Frontiers in Corpus Annotation*, pages 24–31, Boston, Massachusetts, USA, May 2 - May 7. Association for Computational Linguistics.

Adam Meyers, Ruth Reeves, Catherine Macleod, Rachel Szekely, Veronika Zielinska, Brian Young, and Ralph Grishman. 2004b. The cross-breeding of dictionaries. In *Proceedings of LREC-2004*.

Mary Nunes. 1993. Argument linking in english derived nominals. In Robert Van Valin, editor, *Advances in Role and Reference Grammar*, pages 375–432. John Benjamins.

Sebastian Padó, Marco Pennacchiotti, and Caroline Sporleder. 2008. Semantic role assignment for event nominalisations by leveraging verbal data. In *Proceedings of CoLing08*.

Sameer Pradhan, Honglin Sun, Wayne Ward, James H. Martin, and Daniel Jurafsky. 2004. Parsing arguments of nominalizations in english and chinese. In Daniel Marcu Susan Dumais and Salim Roukos, editors, *HLT-NAACL 2004: Short Papers*, pages 141–144, Boston, Massachusetts, USA, May 2 - May 7. Association for Computational Linguistics.

Randolph Quirk, Sidney Greenbaum, Geoffrey Leech, and Jan Svartvik. 1985. *A Comprehensive Grammar of the English Language*. Longman.

Stefan Riezler, Tracy Holloway King, Ronald Kaplan, John T. Maxwell II, Richard Crouch, and Mark Johnson. 2002. Parsing the Wall Street Journal using a Lexical-Functional Grammar and discriminative estimation techniques. In *Proceedings of the ACL'02*.

Scott A. Waterman. 2009. Distributed parse mining. In *Software engineering, testing, and quality assurance for natural language processing (SETQA-NLP 2009)*.

Autosegmental representations in an HPSG of Hausa

Berthold Crysmann
Universität Bonn
Poppelsdorfer Allee 47, D–53115 Bonn
crysmann@ifk.uni-bonn.de

Abstract

In this paper I shall present a treatment of lexical and grammatical tone and vowel length in Hausa, as implemented in an emerging bidirectional HPSG of the language based on the Lingo Grammar Matrix (Bender et al., 2002). I shall argue in particular that a systematic treatment of suprasegmental phonology is indispensible in an implemented grammar of the language, both for theoretical and practical reasons. I shall propose an LKB representation that is strongly inspired by linguistic and computational work on Autosegmental Phonology. Finally, I shall show that the specific implementation presented here is flexible enough to accommodate different levels of suprasegmental information in the input.

1 Introduction

Hausa is a tone language spoken by over 30 million speakers in Northern Nigeria and bordering areas of Niger. Genetically, the language belongs to the Chadic sub-branch of the Afroasiatic family.

In this language, both tone and length are lexically and grammatically distinctive: Hausa distinguishes two vowel lengths, as well as two underlying tones, H(igh) and L(ow). At the surface level, we can observe two level tones, as well as one contour tone (fall). Wolff (1993) cites the following minimal pairs for tone:

(1) a. *fàrī* — 'look (n)'

b. *farī̀* — 'dry season'

c. *farī* — 'white/whiteness'

Rising tone only results from the interaction of grammatical and intonational tone (Sharon Inkelas and Cobler, 1987; Inkelas and Leben, 1990).

In addition to its function of differentiating lexical items, tone is also grammatically distinctive: the paradigms of subjunctive and preterite (=relative completive) TAM markers partially overlap in terms of their segments (*kà* '2sg.subj, *yà* '3sg.m.subj', *tà* '3sg.f.subj' vs. *ka* '2sg.rel.compl, *ya* '3sg.m.rel.compl', *ta* '3sg.f.rel.compl'). Further, the bound possessive linker and the previous reference (=specificity) marker are systematically distinguished by tonal means alone.

(2) a. rī̀ga-r Audù
gown.f-of.f Audù.m
'Audu's gown'

b. rī̀gâ-r
gown.f-spec.f
'the (aforementioned) gown

(3) a. birni-n Kanṑ
town.m-of.m Kano
'Kano town'

b. birnî-n
town.m-spec.m
'the (aforementioned) town'

Similarly, vowel length is also distinctive on both lexical and grammatical levels: Newman (2000) cites the following pair (inter alia): *fāsā̀* 'postpone' vs. *fasā̀* 'smash'. Examples of grammatical length distinctions can again be found in the areas of TAM marking: in relative clauses and focus constructions, completive aspect is expressed by means of the relative completive set (or preterite), using short vowel *na* '1.sg.rel.compl, *ka* '2.sg.rel.compl', *ya* '3.sg.m.rel.compl' and *ta* '3.sg.f.rel.compl', inter alia, which contrasts with the long vowel absolute completive *nā*, *kā*, *yā*, and *tā* used elsewhere (see Jaggar (2006) for discussion of the use of the preterite in narratives). Furthermore, Hausa uses verb-final vowel length to signal presence of a following in-situ direct object (Hayes, 1990; Crysmann, 2005).

Despite the fact that the sophisticated models of suprasegmental phonology developed more than a quarter of a century ago within Autosegmental

Proceedings of the 2009 Workshop on Grammar Engineering Across Frameworks, ACL-IJCNLP 2009, pages 28–36,
Suntec, Singapore, 6 August 2009.

Theory (Goldsmith, 1976; Leben, 1973) have already been rigorously formalised in the nineties in the context of feature-structure-based computational phonology (Bird, 1995; Scobbie, 1991; Bird and Klein, 1994; Walther, 1999), the representation of tone and length has received little or no attention in the area of grammar engineering. This may be partly due to the fact that the languages for which substantial grammars have been developed are not tone languages. Existing grammar implementations of tone languages like Chinese (Fang and King, 2007) do not appear to make use of autosegmental models either, possibly because the assignment of tone in an isolating language is not as intimately connected to inflectional and derivational processes, as it is in a morphologically rich language like Hausa.

In this paper, I shall argue that the issue of suprasegmental phonology is an integral part of any implemented grammar of Hausa, not only from the point of view of linguistic adequacy, but also under grammar-engineering and application-oriented perspectives. I shall propose a treatment of tone and length in an LKB-grammar of Hausa that systematically builds on separate representations of segments, tone and length and discuss how various salient aspects of Hausa syntax and morphology can be addressed using a representation inspired by Autosegmental Theory. Furthermore, I shall address how different levels of suprasegmental information encoded in the different writing systems employed in the language can be robustly integrated into a single grammar, and explore its application potential.

2 Suprasegmental information in Hausa writing systems

2.1 Latin script

2.1.1 Standard orthography (Boko)

Modern Hausa is standardly written using (a modified version of) the Latin script, called *bōkòo*. In addition to the standard 26 letters of the Latin alphabet, Boko uses hooked letters, the apostrophe, as well as digraphs to represent glottalised consonants (ɓ, ɗ, ƙ, ts [s'], 'y [ʔj], ' [ʔ]). Yet, neither tone nor length are represented in the standard orthography.

2.1.2 Tone & length in scientific and educational literature

In contrast to the standard orthography, tone and length are typically fully represented in the academic literature on Hausa. Besides reference grammars and other scientific publications on the language, this includes lexica, some of which exist in machine-readable form (e.g., the on-line version of Bargery (1934) at `http://bargeryhausa.gotdns.com/`).

Length in scientific publications is typically marked using one of the following strategies: diacritical marking of long (macron or post-fixed colon; Newman (2000; Jaggar (2001)) or short vowels (ogonek; Newman and Ma Newman (1977)), and segmental gemination of vowels (long) (Wolff, 1993). Regardless of whether the strategy is diacritic or segmental, there is a strong tendency to have short vowels unmarked, representing the length information on long vowels only.

Tone, by contrast, is exclusively marked by means of diacritics: again, two systems are typically used, one marking low tone with a grave accent leaving high tone unmarked, the other marking high tone with an acute accent, leaving low tone unmarked. Besides that, fully toned representations can also occasionally be found (using acute and grave accents). Falling tone, which phonologically corresponds to a H-L contour associated with a single heavy syllable, is standardly marked with a circumflex accent. Rising tone, by contrast, which only ever plays a role in intonational phonology, as mentioned in section 1, is typically not represented.[1]

Apart from the scientific literature, full representation of suprasegmental information is also provided in most of the Hausa language teaching literature, e.g. Cowan and Schuh (1976; Jungraithmayr et al. (2004). Conventions tend to follow those found in the scientific literature, given that Hausa language teaching often forms an integral part of African linguistics curricula.

The marking strategy assumed in this paper follows the one found in Newman (2000) and Jaggar (2001), using diacritics for low and falling tones, taking high tone as the default. Long vowels are marked by a macron.

2.2 Arabic script (Ajami)

Besides the now standard Latin orthography, Hausa has been written traditionally using a slightly modified version of the Arabic script called *àjàmi*. Today, Ajami is still used occasionally, mainly in the context of religious texts.

Just like Boko, Ajami does not represent tone. Owing to the Semitic origin of the script, however, length distinctions are indeed captured: while short vowels are solely marked by diacritics, if at all, long vowels are represented using a combination of letters and diacritics: long front vowels (/i:/ and /e:/) using the letter *ya* (ي), otherwise used for the palatal glide /j/, long back vowels using the letter *wau* (و), also used for the labio-velar glide /w/, and

[1] Lexical L-H sequences associated with a single syllable undergo tonological simplification rules (Leben, 1971; Newman, 1995).

long /a:/ being represented by alif (ا).[2] Vowel quality (/i:/ vs. /e:/ and /o:/ vs. /u:/) is differentiated by means of diacritics.

Thus, depending on the writing system, different levels of suprasegmental information need to be processed, ranging from full representation in scientific and educational texts, over partial representation (Ajami), to complete absence of any tone or length marking (Ɓoko). This means that the grammar should be able to extract what information is available, and robustly deal with both specified and underspecified input. This is even more important, if we want to include applications, where input in parsing is an underspecified representation, but output in generation requires full specification of suprasegmentals, e.g., in TTS or CALL scenarios.

3 Morphology and suprasegmental phonology

Hausa morphological processes, like derivation and inflection, display close interaction between segmental and suprasegmental marking. Affixation in Hausa is predominantly suffixal, although prefixes and circumfixes are also attested. On the segmental level, affixes can be divided into fully specified suffixes, and reduplicative suffixes. Although partial and full reduplication of entire CV-sequences can also be observed, probably the most common reduplicative pattern involves reduplication and gemination of root consonants, with vowel melodies prespecified.

Tonally, affixes fall into one of three categories: affixes lexically unspecified for tone (only prefixes), tone-integrating affixes (suffixes only) and non-integrating affixes[3]. While non-integrating affixes only specify their own lexical tone, possibly affecting the segmental and suprasegmental realisation of a preceding syllable, tone-integrating suffixes holistically assign a tonal melody to the entire word they attach to.

In contrast to tone, which is often assigned to the entire morphological word, alternations in length do not tend to affect the entire base, but rather only syllables at morpheme boundaries.

3.1 Tone-integrating suffixes

Hausa plurals represent the prototypical case of tone-integrating affixation. The language has an extremely rich set of morphological patterns for plural formation: Newman (2000) identifies 15 classes, many of which have between 2 and 6 subclasses. Quite a few Hausa nouns form the plural according to more than one pattern. Among these 15 plural classes, three are particularly productive, most notably classes 1-3. All these three classes are tone integrating, as are almost all plural formation patterns. Thus, regardless of the tonal specification in the singular, plural formation assigns a regular tone melody to the entire word:

(4) -ōXī (H) (Class I)

a. gulā̀ (HL) — gulōlī 'drum stick'

b. tāgā̀ (HL) — tāgōgī 'window'

c. gyàlè (LL) — gyalōlī 'shawl'

d. tàmbayā̀ (LHL) — tambayōyī 'question'

e. kamfànī (HLH) — kamfanōnī 'company'

f. kwàmìtî (LLHL) — kwamitōcī 'committee'

(5) -ai (LH) (Class II)

a. àlhajī̀ (LHL) — àlhā̀zai 'Hadji'

b. ɗālìbī (HLH) — ɗā̀lìbai 'pupil'

c. sankacḕ (HHL) — sànkàtai 'reaped corn laid down in a row'

d. àlmùbazzàrī (LLHLH) — àlmùbàzzàrai 'spendthrift'

Class I plural formation involves affixation of a partially reduplicative suffix *-ōXī* replacing the base-final vowel, if there is one. Tone in class I plurals is all H, regardless of whether the base is HL, LH, LL, HLH, or LHL. Length specifications, by contrast are carried over from the base, except of course for the base-final vowel. The quality of the affix-internal consonant is determined by reduplication of the base-final consonant, possibly undergoing regular palatalisation.

Class II plurals are formed by means of the fully specified suffix *-ai*, with an associated integrating LH. Tone assignment in Hausa is right to left: thus, L automatically spreads to the left. Again, the tonal shape of the base gets entirely overridden by the LH plural pattern. Non-final length specifications, however, are identical between the singular and the plural.

3.2 Toneless prefixes

As we have seen above, tonal association in Hausa proceeds from right to left. As a result, suffixes carry a lexical specification for tone. Amongst

[2] Ajami letter names are the Hausa equivalent of original Arabic names. For a more complete description of Ajami, see Newman (2000, pp. 729–740).

[3] Among the non-integrating affixes, there is a subclass bearing polar tone, i.e., the surface tone is opposite to that of the neighbouring syllable.

Hausa prefixes, however, one must distinguish between those prefixes carrying a (non-integrating) lexical tone specification themselves, and those prefixes which are inherently unspecified for tone but have their surface tone determined by means of automatic spreading. An example of a prefix of the latter type is provided by the reduplicative prefixes C_1VC_1- and C_1VC_2 found with pluractional verbs. These prefixes consists of an initial consonant that copies the first consonant of the base, followed by a short vowel copying the first vowel of the base (possibly undergoing centralisation). The prefix-final consonant either forms a geminate with the following base-initial consonant, or else copies the second consonant of the base.

(6) C_1VC_1-

a. darnàcē (HLH) — daddarnàcē (HHLH) 'press down/oppress (gr 1)'

b. karàntā (HLH) — kakkaràntā (HHLH) 'read (gr 1)'

c. dā̀gurā̀ (LHL) — dàddā̀gurā̀ (LLHL) 'gnaw at (gr 2)'

d. gyā̀ru (LH) — gyàggyā̀ru (LLH) 'be well repaired (gr 7)'

With trisyllabic bases, it is evident that the tone assumed by the prefix is just a copy of the initial tone of the base.

The tonal pattern assigned to Hausa verbs are determined by paradigm membership, the so-called grade (Parsons, 1960), together with the number of syllables. Tone melodies range from monotonal, over bitonal, to maximally tritonal patterns. Thus, tone-assignment to quadrisyllabic verbs, as derived by pluractional prefixes, is an effect of automatic spreading.

Pluractional affixation to bisyllabic verbs constitutes a slightly more complicated case: Since some paradigms assign different tone melodies to bisyllabic and trisyllabic verbs, prefixation to bisyllabic bases triggers a change in tonal pattern. Note, however, that the tonal pattern assigned to the derived trisyllabic pluractional verb is just the one expected for trisyllabic underived verbs of the same paradigm (cf. underived grade 1 *karàntā* and grade 2 *dā̀gurā̀* above to the pluractional grade 1 and grade 2 verbs below).

(7) a. tākā̀ (HL) — tattā̀kā (HLH) 'step on (gr 1)'

b. jḕfā (LH) — jàjjēfā̀ (LHL) 'throw at (gr 2)'[4]

[4]Owing to the inherent shortness of the reduplicated vowel, long /e:/ and /o:/ undergo regular reduction to [a] in the reduplicant.

Thus, instead of the affix carrying lexical tone, tone is rather assigned holistically to the entire derived word (Newman, 2000).

3.3 Non-integrating affixes

The third class of affixes we shall discuss are lexically specified for tone again (if vocalic). Yet, in contrast to tone-integrating suffixes, they do not override the entire tonal specification of the base. Examples of tonally non-integrating *suffixes* are manifold. They include nominal and verbal suffixes like the bound accusative (polar) and genitive pronouns, the genitive linker (*-n/-r*), the inherently low-tone specificity marker (*-ǹ/-r̀*), and the regular gerundive suffix *-`wā*, among many others. What is common to all these suffixes is that they only affect the segmental and suprasegmental specification of the immediately preceding base-final syllable.

Regular gerunds of verbs in grades 1, 4, 5, 6 and 7 are formed by affixation of a floating tone-initial suffix *-`wā*. When attached to a verb ending in a long high syllable, the base final high tone and the floating low tone combine into a falling contour tone. If the base ends in a high short syllable, as in grade 7, or if the base-final vowel is already low, no tonal change to the base can be observed.

(8) a. karàntā — karàntâwā 'read (gr1)'

b. sayar — sayârwā 'sell (gr5)'

c. kāwō — kāwôwā 'come (gr6)'

d. kāmā̀ — kāmā̀wā 'catch (gr1)'

e. gyā̀ru — gyā̀ruwā 'be repaired (gr7)'

Note that apart from tonal change of high long to falling, the base undergoes no segmental or length change.

Consonantal suffixes, like the genitive linker and the specificity marker, by contrast, necessarily integrate into the coda of the preceding syllable. Since Hausa does not allow long vowels in closed syllables, base-final long vowels and diphthongs are shortened. The specificity marker is identical to the genitive linker, as far as truncation of long vowels and diphthongs is concerned. It differs from the genitive linker, in that it is inherently specified as low, giving rise to a falling tone with high-final bases. With low-final bases, no tonal change can be observed.

(9) a. ƙwai — ƙwa-n-tà '(her) egg'

b. rī̀gā — rī̀ga-r-tà '(her) gown'

c. mōtā̀ — mōtà-r-tà '(her) car'

(10) a. ƙwai — ƙwâ-n 'the (aforementioned) egg'

b. rī̀gā — rī̀gâ-r ‘the (aforementioned) gown’

c. mōtā̀ — mōtà-r ‘(her) car’

Note that in contrast to tone-integrating suffixes, segmental and suprasegmental changes are strictly local, affecting material in adjacent syllables only.

Besides non-integrating suffixes there are some very rare prefixes that can be regarded as inherently specified for tone. One such prefix is low tone bà- that features in singular ethnonyms, like, e.g. *bàhaushḕ* ‘Hausa person’. Typically, the prefix bà- is accompanied by a final tone-integrating HL suffix *-ḕ* (masc) or HLH *-ā/-ìyā* (fem), but not always. With regular ethnonyms, the initial tone of the suffix (H) spreads to the left, up to but excluding the low tone prefix. The plural of such ethnonyms is formed without a prefix. Instead, a tone-integrating H or LH suffix *-āwā* is used. Vowel length of the base is retained throughout:

(11) Fàransà ‘France’ — Bàfaranshḕ (m), Bàfaranshìyā (f) , Faransāwā (pl) ‘French’

(12) Jāmùs ‘Germany’ — Bàjāmushḕ (m), Bàjāmushìyā (f) , Jāmusāwā (pl) ‘French’

Besides the regular pattern, there are a few ethnonyms that use a non-integrating *-ī* e.g. *Bàgṑbirī* from *Gṑbir*, thus preserving the tonal pattern of the place name base. According to Newman (2000), however, many Hausa speakers prefer to use the regular tone-integrating suffix *-ḕ* instead. Thus, entirely non-integrating formation of ethnonyms has ceased to be a part of productive Hausa morphology.

Moreover, even the productivity of tonally specified *bà-* seems to be diminished: while the plural is still productive, new ethnonyms tend to be formed using alternate periphrastic constructions *ɗan/mùtumìn* ‘son/man of’ (Newman, 2000).

(13) a. Pàlàsɗīnù ‘Palestine’ — ɗan/mùtumìn Pàlàsɗīnù (m) — Palasɗīnāwā (pl) ‘Palestinian’

b. Bosniyà ‘Bosnia’ — ɗan/mùtumìn Bosniyà (m) — Bosniyāwā (pl) ‘Bosnian’

To summarise, I shall take integrating and non-integrating suffixation as the standard case in Hausa, together with toneless prefixation. As we shall see in the description of our implementation in the following section, the treatment of isolated cases of tonally specified prefixes will be treated as a non-productive sub-regularity.

4 Representing autosegmental phonology in the LKB

4.1 Orthographemics in the LKB

The LKB (Copestake, 2002) has built-in support for orthographemic alternations, providing support for inflectional and derivational morphology. Technically, the orthographemic component of the LKB adopts a string-unification approach. Below is an example of the spelling part of regular -ōXī plural formation, together with the definitions of letter sets and wild-cards used. Patterns on the right pre-empt patterns further to the left.

(14)
```
%(wild-card (?v aeiou))
%(letter-set (!c bcdfghjklmnpqrstvwxyzɓɗƙƴ))
noun_pl1_vow_ir :=
   %suffix (!c?v !co!ci) (t?v toci)
   (s?v soshi) (w?v woyi) (ts?v tsotsi)
   noun-plural-infl-rule &
   ...
```

In the above rule, the letter set `!c` is string unified with the corresponding consonantal letter in the input. Note that in contrast to wild cards (e.g. `?v`), multiple occurrences of letter set identifiers within the same pattern are bound to the same consonant, providing a convenient solution to gemination and partial reduplication.

Orthographemic rules are unary (lexical) rules consisting of a feature structure description and an associated spelling change. The orthographemic part is applied to surface tokens in order to derive potential stem forms. The parser’s chart is then initialised with lexical entries that have a corresponding stem form. The orthographemic rules that have been applied in order to derive the stem are recorded on an agenda such that the feature structure part can be applied to the lexical entries thus retrieved.

Recall from section 2 that Hausa standard orthography does not represent tone or length. Thus, suprasegmentally unmarked strings define the common denominator for retrieving entries from the lexicon. But even if the input is marked diacritically for suprasegmentals, tone-integrating morphology can lead to drastic tonal changes, which are superficially encoded as segmental alternations (since á $\neq$ à). Moreover, we hope to have shown above that tone and segmental phonology should best be treated separately. Consequently, orthographic representations unmarked for tone constitute the common denominator for all orthographic input representations.

In a first preprocessing step, tone and length specifications on input tokens are extracted by means of a regular expression preprocessing engine built into the LKB (Waldron et al., 2006).

Instead of simply removing this potentially valuable information, the preprocessor rules convert the (diacritical) marking of tone and length into an inverse suffixal representation, separated from the segmental string by _. Overtly marked high will be represented as _H, overtly marked low as _L, and lack of tonal marking is recorded as _*. Similarly, length information, if present, will be recorded by means of a colon next to the corresponding tone. E.g., input `ɗàlìbai` 'pupils' will be converted into `ɗalibai_*_L_L:`, whereas tonally unspecified `ɗalibai` will become `ɗalibai_*_*_*`. Input partially specified for length (`ɗaalibai`), as, e.g., in Ajami, will receive a representation as `ɗalibai_*_*_*:`.

Once we have separated suprasegmental information from the orthography proper and stored it in the form of suffixal annotations, we can use LKB's standard orthographemic machinery to convert the suffixal annotation into feature structure constraints.[5]

4.2 Phonological representation

As we have seen above, there are several strategies of tone and length marking in Hausa. While overtly marked tone and length is both unambiguous in itself and directly enables us to infer what marking strategy is used, the interpretation of vowels unmarked for tone or length depends entirely on the context: if a low-marking strategy is employed, unmarked segments (=_*) can be interpreted as high. However, if no marking of tone occurs at all in the input, unmarked segments should be compatible with any tone. The very same goes for length. In order to enable the grammar to flexibly infer the meaning of these underspecified annotations, we introduce the following type hierarchy of tonal marking. The only assumption made here is that the marking strategy being adopted is used consistently across the entire input sentence.[6]

Lexical and grammatical tones will be one of *high*, *low*, or *fall*.[7] In addition to these three linguistic tones, the type hierarchy features tonal types that correspond to tonal annotations found in the input: *utone* is the type associated with tonally unmarked syllables, *tone_* is the type associated with a high-marking strategy, *_tone* corresponds to low-marking, and *_tone_* to full tonal marking (overt high and low).

(15)

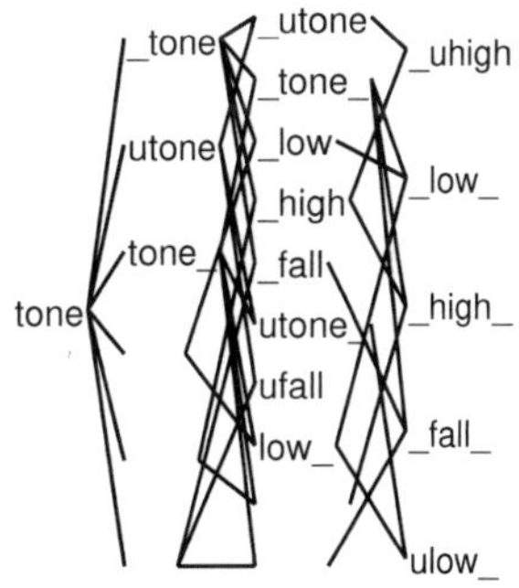

Depending on which annotations are present in the input, the meaning of underspecified annotations can be determined on the basis of type inference. The orthographemic rules that consume tonal annotations do exactly two things: first, they record the tone specification just found as the first member of the TONE list of the daughter, successfully building up a list of surface tones from right to left.

(16)
```
_HH_ir :=
  %suffix (* _H:)
  diacritic-irule &
  [SUPRA [TONE [LIST #tones,
                LAST #tl],
          LEN  [LIST #lens,
                LAST #ll]],
   DTR [SUPRA [TONE [LIST
            high-marked-list &
            <high . #tones>,
                     LAST #last],
               LEN  [LIST
            long-marked-list &
            <long . #lens>,
                     LAST #ll]]]].

_*_ir :=
  %suffix (* \*)
  diacritic-irule &
  [SUPRA [TONE [LIST #tones,
                LAST #tl],
          LEN  [LIST #lens,
                LAST #ll]],
   DTR [SUPRA [TONE [LIST
            <utone . #tones>,
                     LAST #last],
               LEN  [LIST
            <ulength . #lens>,
                     LAST #ll]]]].
```

If the annotation is that of an overtly unmarked tone, the underspecified type *utone* is inserted, otherwise *high* or *low*, as appropriate. H or L tone rules simultaneously constrain the entire tone list according to the marking strategy, using list constraints.

(17)
```
high-marked-list :=
  tone-marked-list.
high-marked-null :=
  high-marked-list &
  tone-marked-null.
```

[5] In the near future, we plan to supplant this two-step solution with a direct conversion of using diacritical information into feature structure annotations, using the advanced token-mapping developed by Adolphs et al. (2008). At present, however, this token-mapping has only been integrated into the Pet run-time system (Callmeier, 2000), but not yet into the LKB.

[6] In principle, even this assumption can be relaxed, at the peril of having reduced cross-sentence disambiguation.

[7] I do not decompose falling tone into HL sequences, thereby simplifying the alignment between tone specifications, length specifications and segments.

```
high-marked-cons :=
  high-marked-list &
  tone-marked-cons &
  [FIRST tone_,
   REST high-marked-list].
```

Presence of a single overtly marked high tone will constrain every element of the tone list to be a subtype of *high_*. According to the hierarchy of tonal types given above, the greatest lower bound of *utone* and *high_* however, is *low_*, denoting (unmarked) low tone under a high-marking strategy. Thus, whatever tonal marking is found, unmarked tones are coerced to represent the opposite tones. The way the type hierarchy is set up, 4 different marking strategies are possible: completely unspecified tone, high-tone marking, low-tone marking and fully explicit high- and low-tone marking.

With the constraints we have just seen, we only get disambiguation of unmarked tone (and length) within the same word. In order to disambiguate across the entire sentence, we use difference lists of these tone and length lists to propagate the marking regime to preceding and following words. In essence, we use two difference lists _LTONE and _RTONE to propagate from left to right and vice versa.[8] Lexically, every word inserts its own tone list as the singleton member of each difference list. The general phrasal types from which all grammar rules inherit now concatenate the _LTONE and _RTONE values of their daughters left to right and right to left, respectively.

The tone marking rules given above are then further constrained according to the types of _LTONE and _RTONE. Using list-of-list type constraints as given below, every word marked for tone will constrain the marking regime found to its left and to its right.

(18)
```
hm-llist := tm-llist.
hm-clist := tm-clist &
    hm-llist &
    [FIRST high-marked-list,
     REST hm-llist].
hm-nlist := hm-llist & tm-nlist.
```

The treatment of length marking, as we have hinted at already, is entirely analogous to that of tone, imposing the corresponding constraints on a list of vowel length specifications.

With these constraints in place, we get the following disambiguation results (note that the verb *zō* is lexically specified as long):

(19) a. Fully unspecified: `Ya zo` (3 readings: *yā zō, ya zō, yà zō*)

b. Length specified: `Ya zoo` (2 readings: *ya zō, yà zō*)

c. Length specified: `Yaa zoo` (1 reading: yā zō)

d. Tone/length specified: `Ya kaawoo shì` (1 reading: *ya kāwō shì*)

e. Fully specified: `Yá zóó` (1 reading: *ya zō*)

f. Inconsistent: `Yaa zo` (0 readings)

As witnessed above, presence of length marking coerces vowels not marked as long into the short vowel reading. Similarly, presence of a single low tone marking enforces a high tone reading of overtly unmarked tones.

In generation, the grammar only uses fully specified tone marking, i.e., application of rules such as `_*_ir` is blocked. As a result, we always get a surface representation with full tone and length information. Post-generation Lisp functions are used to convert the suffixal notation into the appropriate diacritic format.

4.3 Morphology

The main motivation for having tone and length represented on separate lists is two-fold: first, as witnessed by Ajami, writing systems may overtly mark one distinction but not the other. Second, and more importantly, we have seen in section 3, that morphological processes tend to leave length intact, even if the entire word is holistically marked with a completely new tonal melody, unrelated to that of the base. Having two separate lists, we can replace the tonal structure in the course of morphological derivation but still have the rhythmic structure shared between base and derived form by means of reentrancies.

Here we investigate in more detail the role these representations play in morphological derivation.

In the previous section, we provided a general representation of segmental and suprasegmental information, the latter being encoded by means of two lists and showed how preprocessor rules and orthographemic rules are used to extract this information from the input and associate it with parts of the feature structure, such that it can be matched against morphological and lexical constraints on length and tone.

Since both tone and length are lexically distinctive, every lexical item specifies the contents of its SUPRA|TONE and SUPRA|LEN lists. The order of the elements on these two lists is right to left, facilitating a treatment of tone spreading by means of list types. At the same time, this encoding provides convenient access to the right-most length and tone

[8] Since only overtly marked items can disambiguate tonally unmarked ones, and the position of these disambiguating items in the string is not known a priori, we need two lists of lists, one for disambiguation of preceding material (_LTONE), the other for following material _RTONE.

specification. Since Hausa is predominantly suffixal, non-holistic morphophonological changes to tone and length specifications exclusively target the right-most syllable of the base.

As we have observed above, tonal changes can be far more global than segmental and length alternations. Thus, we will use the LEN list to synchronise the segmental and suprasegmental representations. Consequently, length specifications will always be a closed list. Tone, by contrast, may involve spreading, i.e. the exact number of individual H of an all H tone melody is determined by the number of available tone bearing units, which corresponds to vowel length specifications in our grammar. Since the number of tone bearing units is already fixed by the length of LEN, and because the tone marking rules operate synchronously on TONE and LEN, we are free to underspecify the tonal representation as to the exact length of the melody. Therefore, we can provide a straightforward account of right-to-left association and left-ward tone spreading in terms of open tone list types.

(20)
```
h*-list := list.
h*-cons := h*-list &
           cons & [FIRST high,
   REST h*-list].

h*-null := h*-list & null.

h*-l-list := list.
h*-l-cons := h*-l-list &
             cons & [FIRST low,
                     REST h*-list].
```

As we shall see shortly, these list types provide a highly general way to constrain holistic tonal assignment, independently of the segmental makeup of the base.

In order to illustrate the interplay between segmental and suprasegmental constraints in morphological derivation, I provide a treatment of the two major types of morphological rules: tone-integrating and non-integrating.[9]

(21)
```
noun_pl1_vow_ir :=
%suffix (!c?v !co!ci) ...
noun-plural-infl-rule  \&
[SUPRA
   [TONE [LIST h*-list],
    LEN [LIST < long, long . #l1>,
         LAST #llast] ],
 DTR [SYNSEM.LKEYS.--MCLASS n-pl-1,
      SUPRA.LEN [LIST  < [] . #l1>,
                 LAST #llast]]].
```

Tone integrating affixes In our discussion of the Class I plural inflection rule above, we have only specified the segmental changes. As detailed in the version below, holistic assignment of tone is achieved by means of a list type constraint on the TONE of the mother, paired with the absence of any tonal restrictions regarding the morphological daughter (the base). The length marking of the two inherently long suffix vowels is captured by means of the addition of two *long* specification at the front of LEN. Affixation of *-ōXī* replaces the base final vowel. Accordingly, the associated initial length specification of the daughter is skipped and the remaining list is passed on to the length specification of the mother.

Non-integrating affixes In feminine singular specificity marking, both non-integrating tone and length changes can be observed. As depicted below, high-final bases undergo a tone change to fall. The remainder of the TONE list is structure-shared between mother and daughter, carrying over any list constraints that might be imposed there.

(22)
```
f-sg-noun_def_high_ir :=
 %suffix (!v !vr) (!vi !vr) ...
 noun-def-f-sg-irule &
 [SUPRA [TONE [LIST <fall . #tl >,
                LAST #tlast],
          LEN [LIST <short . #l1>,
               LAST #llast]],
  DTR [SUPRA
        [TONE [LIST <high . #tl>,
               LAST #tlast],
          LEN [LIST <[] . #l1>,
               LAST #llast] ]]].
```

Likewise, final shortening, which is triggered by the affixation of a syllable-final consonant, is captured by an analogous constraint on LEN.

5 Conclusion

In this paper, we have proposed a treatment of tone and length in Hausa in terms of distinct representations of segments, tone and length. We have shown that this separation is not only needed to accommodate different orthographic representations in the input, but that it also paves the way for a more general account of Hausa morphology, most notably holistic assignment of tonal melodies combined with tone spreading. At present, the grammar is not only capable of extracting different levels of suprasegmental annotations contained in the input, but can also resolving tone and length ambiguities on the basis of grammatical constraints: e.g., the ambiguity between genitive linker and previous reference marker, or the ambiguity between subjunctive, preterite, and absolute completive in relative and focus constructions. In the future, we intend to equip the grammar with parse selection models, to further enhance disambiguation. Given the bidirectionality of the grammar and its flexible support for tone and length, we plan to use it in the context of TTS and CALL applications in the near future.

[9]Toneless prefixation with automatic spreading constitutes just a special sub-case of tone-integrating rules.

References

Peter Adolphs, Stephan Oepen, Ulrich Callmeier, Berthold Crysmann, Dan Flickinger, and Bernd Kiefer. 2008. Some fine points of hybrid natural language parsing. In *Proceedings of the 6th Conference on Language Resources and Evaluation (LREC 2008), May, Marrakesh.*

G. P. Bargery. 1934. *A Hausa–English Dictionary and English–Hausa Vocabulary*. Oxford University Press, London.

Emily M. Bender, Dan Flickinger, and Stephan Oepen. 2002. The grammar matrix: An open-source starter-kit for the rapid development of cross-linguistically consistent broad-coverage precision grammar. In John Carroll, Nelleke Oostdijk, and Richard Sutcliffe, editors, *Proceedings of the Workshop on Grammar Engineering and Evaluation at the 19th International Conference on Computational Linguistics*, pages 8–14.

Steven Bird and Ewan Klein. 1994. Phonological analysis in typed feature systems. *Computational Linguistics*, 20(3):455–491.

Steven Bird. 1995. *Computational Phonology. A Constraint-based Approach.* Studies in Natural Language Processing. Cambridge University Press, Cambridge.

Ulrich Callmeier. 2000. PET — a platform for experimentation with efficient HPSG processing techniques. *Journal of Natural Language Engineering*, 6(1):99–108.

Ann Copestake. 2002. *Implementing Typed Feature Structure Grammars.* CSLI Publications, Stanford.

J. Ronayne Cowan and Russell Schuh. 1976. *Spoken Hausa*. Spoken Language Services, Ithaca.

Berthold Crysmann. 2005. An inflectional approach to Hausa final vowel shortening. In Geert Booij and Jaap van Marle, editors, *Yearbook of Morphology 2004*, pages 73–112. Kluwer.

Ji Fang and Tracy Holloway King. 2007. An LFG Chinese grammar for machine use. In Tracy Holloway King and Emily Bender, editors, *Proceedings of the GEAF 2007 Workshop*, CSLI Studies in Computational Linguistics ONLIN. CSLI Publications.

John A. Goldsmith. 1976. *Autosegmental Phonology.* Ph.D. thesis, MIT.

Bruce Hayes. 1990. Precompiled phrasal phonology. In Sharon Inkelas and Draga Zec, editors, *The Phonology-Syntax Connection*, pages 85–108. University of Chicago Press.

Sharon Inkelas and William R. Leben. 1990. Where phonology and phonetics intersect: The case of Hausa intonation. In Mary E. Beckman and John Kingston, editors, *Between the Grammar and the Physics of Speech*, Papers in Laboratory Phonology, pages 17–34. Cambridge University Press, New York.

Philip Jaggar. 2001. *Hausa*. John Benjamins, Amsterdam.

Philip Jaggar. 2006. The Hausa perfective tense-aspect used in wh-/focus constructions and historical narratives: A unified account. In Larry Hyman and Paul Newman, editors, *West African Linguistics: Descriptive, Comparative, and Historical Studies in Honor of Russell G. Schuh*, Studies in African Linguistics, pages 100–133.

Herrmann Jungraithmayr, Wilhelm J. G. Möhlig, and Anne Storch. 2004. *Lehrbuch der Hausa-Sprache.* Rüdiger Köppe Verlag, Köln.

William R. Leben. 1971. The morphophonemics of tone in Hausa. In C.-W. Kim and Herbert Stahlke, editors, *Papers in African Linguistics*, pages 201–218. Linguistic Research, Edmonton.

William Leben. 1973. *Suprasegmental Phonology.* Ph.D. thesis, MIT.

Paul Newman and Roxana Ma Newman. 1977. *Modern Hausa–English Dictionary.* University Press, Ibadan and Zaria, Nigeria.

Paul Newman. 1995. Hausa tonology: Complexities in an 'easy' tone language. In John Goldsmith, editor, *The Handbook of Phonological Theory*, pages 762–781. Blackwell, Oxford.

Paul Newman. 2000. *The Hausa Language. An Encyclopedic Reference Grammar.* Yale University Press, New Haven, CT.

F. W. Parsons. 1960. The verbal system in Hausa. *Afrika und Übersee*, 44:1–36.

Jim Scobbie. 1991. *Attribute-Value Phonology.* Ph.D. thesis, University of Edinburgh.

William R. Leben Sharon Inkelas and Mark Cobler. 1987. The phonology of intonation in Hausa. In *Proceedings of the North-Eastern Linguistic Society 17*, pages 327–341.

Ben Waldron, Ann Copestake, Ulrich Schäfer, and Bernd Kiefer. 2006. Preprocessing and tokenisation standards in DELPH-IN tools. In *Proceedings of the 5th International Conference on Language Resources and Evaluation (LREC-2006)*, pages 2263–2268, Genova, May.

Markus Walther. 1999. *Deklarative Prosodische Morphologie*, volume 399 of *Linguistische Arbeiten.* Niemeyer, Tübingen.

Ekkehard Wolff. 1993. *Referenzgrammatik des Hausa.* LIT, Münster.

Construction of a German HPSG grammar from a detailed treebank

Bart Cramer[†] **and Yi Zhang**[†‡]
Department of Computational Linguistics & Phonetics, Saarland University, Germany[†]
LT-Lab, German Research Center for Artificial Intelligence, Germany[‡]
{bcramer,yzhang}@coli.uni-saarland.de

Abstract

Grammar extraction in deep formalisms has received remarkable attention in recent years. We recognise its value, but try to create a more precision-oriented grammar, by hand-crafting a core grammar, and learning lexical types and lexical items from a treebank. The study we performed focused on German, and we used the Tiger treebank as our resource. A completely hand-written grammar in the framework of HPSG forms the inspiration for our core grammar, and is also our frame of reference for evaluation. [1]

1 Introduction

Previous studies have shown that treebanks can be helpful when constructing grammars. The most well-known example is PCFG-based statistical parsing (Charniak and Johnson, 2005), where a PCFG is induced from, for instance, the Penn Treebank. The underlying statistical techniques have been refined in the last decade, and previous work indicates that the labelled f-score of this method converges to around 91%.

An alternative to PCFGs, with more linguistic relevance, is formed by deeper formalisms, such as TAG (Joshi and Schabes, 1997), CCG (Steedman, 1996), LFG (Kaplan and Bresnan, 1995) and HPSG (Pollard and Sag, 1994). For LFG (Butt et al., 2002) and HPSG (Flickinger, 2000; Müller, 2002), large hand-written grammars have been developed. In the case of HPSG, the grammar writers found the small number of principles too restrictive, and created more rules (approximately 50 to 300) to accommodate for phenomena that vanilla HPSG cannot describe correctly. The increased linguistic preciseness comes at a cost, though: such grammars have a lower out-of-the-box coverage, i.e. they will not give an analysis on a certain portion of the corpus.

Experiments have been conducted, where a lexicalised grammar is learnt from treebanks, a methodology for which we coin the name *deep grammar extraction*. The basic architecture of such an experiment is to convert the treebank to a format that is compatible with the chosen linguistic formalism, and read off the lexicon from that converted treebank. Because all these formalisms are heavily lexicalised, the core grammars only consist of a small number of principles or operators. In the case of CCG (Hockenmaier and Steedman, 2002), the core grammar consists of the operators that CCG stipulates: function application, composition and type-raising. Standard HPSG defines a few schemata, but these are usually adapted for a large-scale grammar. Miyao et al. (2004) tailor their core grammar for optimal use with the Penn Treebank and the English language, for example by adding a new schema for relative clauses.

Hockenmaier and Steedman (2002), Miyao et al. (2004) and Cahill et al. (2004) show fairly good results on the Penn Treebank (for CCG, HPSG and LFG, respectively): these parsers achieve accuracies on predicate-argument relations between 80% and 87%, which show the feasibility and scalability of this approach. However, while this is a simple method for a highly configurational language like English, it is more difficult to extend to languages with more complex morphology or with word orders that display more freedom. Hockenmaier (2006) is the only study known to the authors that applies this method to German, a language that displays these properties.

This article reports on experiments where the advantages of hand-written and derived grammars

[1]The research reported in this paper has been carried out with financial support from the Deutsche Forschungsgemeinschaft and the German Excellence Cluster of Multimodal Computing & Interaction.

Proceedings of the 2009 Workshop on Grammar Engineering Across Frameworks, ACL-IJCNLP 2009, pages 37–45,
Suntec, Singapore, 6 August 2009.

are combined. Compared to previous deep grammar extraction approaches, a more sophisticated core grammar (in the framework of HPSG) is created. Also, more detailed syntactic features are learnt from the resource treebank, which leads to a more precise lexicon. Parsing results are compared with GG (German Grammar), a previously hand-written German HPSG grammar (Müller, 2002; Crysmann, 2003; Crysmann, 2005).

2 Core grammar

2.1 Head-driven phrase structure grammar

This study has been entirely embedded in the HPSG framework (Pollard and Sag, 1994). This is a heavily lexicalised, constraint-based theory of syntax, and it uses typed feature structures as its representation. HPSG introduces a small number of principles (most notably, the Head Feature Principle) that guide the construction of a few Immediate Dominance schemata. These schemata are meant to be the sole basis to combine words and phrases. Examples of schemata are head-complement, head-subject, head-specifier, head-filler (for long-distance dependencies) and head-modifier.

In this study, the core grammar is an extension of the off-the-shelf version of HPSG. The type hierarchy is organised by a typed feature structure hierarchy (Carpenter, 1992), and can be read by the LKB system (Copestake, 2002) and the PET parser (Callmeier, 2000). The output is given in Minimal Recursion Semantics (Copestake et al., 2005) format, which can be minimally described as a way to include scope information in dependency output.

2.2 The German language

Not unlike English, German uses verb position to distinguish between different clause types. In declarative sentences, verbs are positioned in the second position, while subordinate classes are verb-final. Questions and imperatives are verb-initial. However, German displays some more freedom with respect to the location of subjects, complements and adjuncts: they can be scrambled rather freely. The following sentences are all grammatical, and have approximately the same meaning:

(1) a. Der Präsident hat
The.NOM President.NOM has
gestern das Buch
yesterday the.ACC book.ACC
gelesen.
read.PERF.
'The president read the book yesterday'

b. Gestern hat der Präsident das Buch gelesen.

c. Das Buch hat der Präsident gestern gelesen.

As can be seen, the main verb is placed at second position (the so-called 'left bracket'), but all other verbs remain at the end of the sentence, in the 'right bracket'. Most linguistic theories about German recognise the existence of topological fields: the *Vorfeld* before the left bracket, the *Mittelfeld* between both brackets, and the *Nachfeld* after the right bracket. The first two are mainly used for adjuncts and arguments, whereas the *Nachfeld* is typically, but not necessarily, used for extraposed material (e.g. relative clauses or comparative phrases) and some VPs. Again, the following examples mean roughly the same:

(2) a. Er hat das Buch, das sie
He has the.ACC Book.ACC, that she
empfohlen hat, gelesen.
recommended has, read.PERF.
He has read the book that she recommended.

b. Er hat das Buch gelesen, das sie empfohlen hat.

c. Das Buch hat er gelesen, das sie empfohlen hat.

Another distinctive feature of German is its relatively rich morphology. Nominals are marked with case, gender and number, and verbs with number, person, tense and mood. Adjectives and nouns have to agree with respect to gender, number and declension type, the latter being determined by the (non-)existence and type of determiner used in the noun phrase. Verbs and subjects have to agree with respect to number and person. German also displays highly productive noun compounding, which amplifies the need for effective unknown word handling. Verb particles can either be separated from or concatenated to the verb: compare 'Er schläft aus' ('He sleeps in') and 'Er

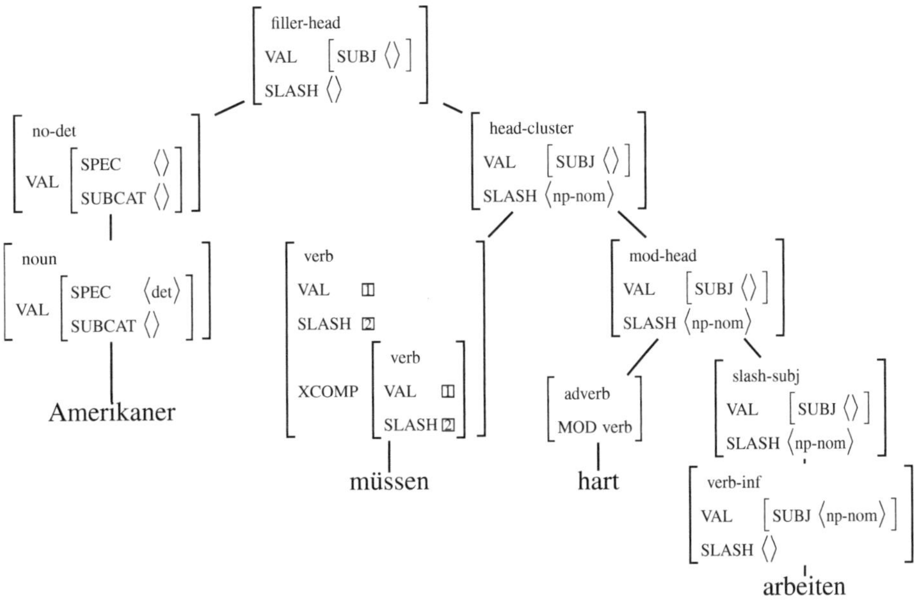

Figure 1: This figure shows a (simplified) parse tree of the sentence 'Amerikaner müssen hart arbeiten' ('Americans have to work hard').

wird ausschlafen' ('He will sleep in'). In such verbs, the word 'zu' (which translates to the English 'to' in 'to sleep') can be infixed as well: 'er versucht auszuschlafen' ('He tries to sleep in').

These characteristics make German a comparatively complex language to parse with CFGs: more variants of the same lemma have to be memorised, and the expansion of production rules will be more diverse, with a less peaked statistical distribution. Efforts have been made to adapt existing CFG models to German (Dubey and Keller, 2003), but the results still don't compare to state-of-the-art parsing of English.

2.3 Structure of the core grammar

The grammar uses the main tenets from Head-driven Phrase Structure Grammar (Pollard and Sag, 1994). However, different from earlier deep grammar extraction studies, more sophisticated structures are added. Müller (2002) proposes a new schema (head-cluster) to account for verb clusters in the right bracket, which includes the possibility to merge subcategorisation frames of e.g. object-control verbs and its dependent verb. Separate rules for determinerless NPs, genitive modification, coordination of common phrases, relative phrases and direct speech are also created.

The free word order of German is accounted for by scrambling arguments with lexical rules, and by allowing adjuncts to be a modifier of unsaturated verb phrases. All declarative phrases are considered to be head-initial, with an adjunct or argument fronted using the SLASH feature, which is then discharged using the head-filler schema. The idea put forward by, among others, (Kiss and Wesche, 1991) that all sentences should be right-branching is linguistically pleasing, but turns out be computationally very expensive (Crysmann, 2003), and the right-branching reading should be replaced by a left-branching reading when the right bracket is empty (i.e. when there is no auxiliary verb present).

An example of a sentence is presented in figure 1. It receives a right-branching analysis, because the infinitive 'arbeiten' resides in the right bracket. The unary rule slash-subj moves the required subject towards the SLASH value, so that it can be discharged in the *Vorfeld* by the head-filler schema. 'müssen' is an example of an argument attraction verb, because it pulls the valence feature (containing SUBJ, SUBCAT etc; not visible in the diagram) to itself. The head-cluster rule assures that the VAL value then percolates upwards. Because 'Amerikaner' does not have a specifier, a separate unary rule (no-det) takes care of discharging the SPEC feature, before it can be combined with the filler-head rule.

As opposed to (Hockenmaier, 2006), this study

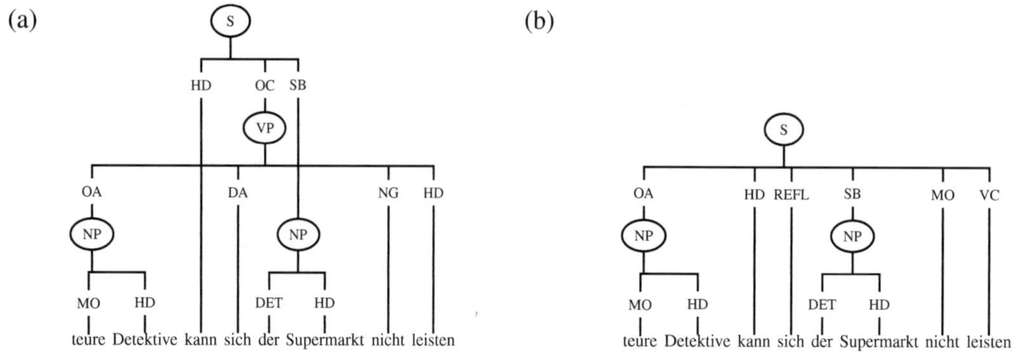

Figure 2: (a) shows the original sentence, whereas (b) shows the sentence after preprocessing. Note that NP is now headed, that the VP node is deleted, and that the verbal cluster is explicitly marked in (b). The glossary of this sentence is 'Expensive.ACC detectives.ACC can REFL the.NOM supermarket.NOM not afford'

employs a core lexicon for words that have marked semantic behaviour. These are usually closed word classes, and include items such as raising and auxiliary verbs, possessives, reflexives, articles, complementisers etc. The size of this core lexicon is around 550 words. Note that, because the core lexicon only contains function words, its coverage is negligible without additional entries.

3 Derivation of the lexicon

3.1 The Tiger treebank

The Tiger treebank (Brants et al., 2002) is a treebank that embraces the concept of constituency, but can have crossing branches, i.e. the tree might be non-projective. This allowed the annotators to capture the German free word order. Around one-third of the sentences received a non-projective analysis. An example can be found in figure 2. Additionally, it annotates each branch with a syntactic function.

The text comes from a German newspaper (Frankfurter Rundschau). It was annotated semi-automatically, using a cascaded HMM model. After each phase of the HMM model, the output was corrected by human annotators. The corpus consists of over 50,000 sentences, with an average sentence length of 17.6 tokens (including punctuation). The treebank employs 26 phrase categories, 56 PoS tags and 48 edge labels. It also encodes number, case and gender at the noun terminals, and tense, person, number and mood at verbs. Whether a verb is finite, an infinitive or a participle is encoded in the PoS tag. A peculiarity in the annotation of noun phrases is the lack of headedness, which was meant to keep the annotation as theory-independent as reasonably possible.

3.2 Preprocessing

A number of changes had to be applied to the treebank to facilitate the read-off procedure:

- A heuristic head-finding procedure is applied in the spirit of (Magerman, 1995). We use priority lists to find the NP's head, determiner, appositions and modifiers. PPs and CPs are also split into a head and its dependent.
- If a verb has a separated verb particle, this particle is attached to the lemma of the verb. For instance, if the verb 'schlafen' has a particle 'aus', the lemma will be turned into 'ausschlafen' ('sleep in'). If this is not done, subcategorisation frames will be attributed to the wrong lemma.
- Sentences with auxiliaries are non-projective, if the adjunct of the embedded VP is in the *Vorfeld*. This can be solved by flattening the tree (removing the VP node), and marking the verbal cluster (VC) explicitly. See figure 2 for an example. 67.6% of the original Tiger treebank is projective, and with this procedure, this is lifted to 80.1%.
- The Tiger treebank annotates reflexive pronouns with the PoS tag PRF, but does not distinguish the syntactic role. Therefore, if a verb has an object that has PRF as its part-of-speech, the label of that edge is changed into REFL, so that reflexive verbs can be found.

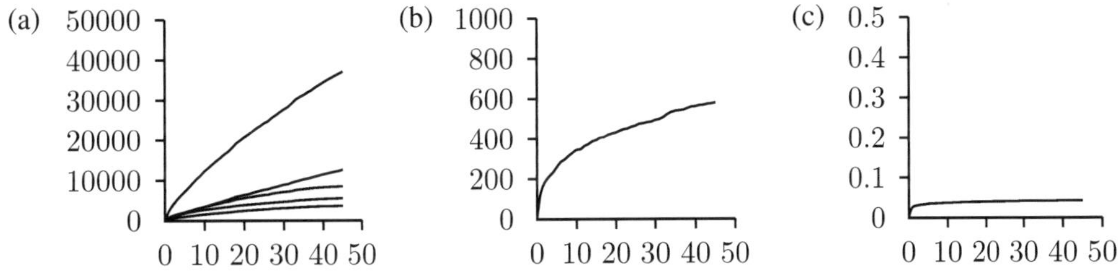

Figure 3: These graphs show learning curves of the algorithm on the first 45,000 sentences of the Tiger treebank. Graph (a) indicates the amount of lemmas learnt (from top to bottom: nouns, names, adjectives, verbs and adverbs). The graph in (b) shows the number of distinct lexical types for verbs that are learnt. Graph (c) shows the average proportion of morphological forms that is observed per verb lemma, assuming that each verb has 28 different forms: infinitive, zu (to) + infinitive, participle, imperative and 24 finite forms (3 (person) * 2 (number) * 2 (tense) * 2 (mood)).

The preprocessing stage failed in 1.1% of the instances.

3.3 Previous work

The method described in Hockenmaier (2006) first converts the Tiger analysis to a tree, after which the lexical types were derived. Because it was the author's goal to convert all sentences, some rather crude actions had to be taken to render non-projective trees projective: whenever a certain node introduces non-projectivity, some of its daughters are moved to the parent tree, until that node is projective. Below, we give two examples where this will lead to incorrect semantic composition, with the consequence of flawed lexicon entries. We argue that it is questionable whether the impressive conversion scores actually represent a high conversion quality. It would be interesting to see how this grammar performs in a real parsing task, but no such study has been carried out so far.

The first case deals with extraposed material in the *Nachfeld*. Typical examples include relative phrases, comparatives and PH/RE constructions[2]. The consequence is that the head of the extraposed material will be connected to the verb, instead of to the genuine head.

Another example where Hockenmaier's algorithm will create incorrect lexical entries is when the edge label is PAR (for 'parentheses') or in the case of appositions. Consider the following sentence:

(3) mit 160 Planstellen (etliche sind
with 160 permanent posts (several are
allerdings noch unbesetzt)
however still unoccupied)

The conclusion that will be drawn from this sentence is that 'sind' can modify nouns, which is only true due to the parentheses, and has no relation with the specific characteristics of 'sind'. Similarly, appositions will act as modifiers of nouns. Although one might argue that this is the canonical CCG derivation for these phenomena, it is not in the spirit of the HPSG grammars, and we believe that these constructions are better handled in rules than in the lexicon.

3.4 Procedure

In our approach, we will be more conservative, and the algorithm will only add facts to its knowledge base if the evidence is convincing. That means that less Tiger graphs will get projective analyses, but that doesn't have to be a curse: we can derive lexical types from non-projective analyses just as well, and leave the responsibility for solving the more complex grammatical phenomena to the core grammar. For example, lexical rules will deal with fronting and *Mittelfeld* scrambling, as we have stated before. This step of the

[2]NPs, AVPs and PPs can, instead of their usual headed structure, be divided in two parts: a 'placeholder' and a 'repeated element'. These nodes often introduce non-projectivity, and it is not straightforward to create a valid linguistic analysis for these phenomena. Example sentences of these categories (NPs, AVPs and PPs, respectively) are:

(1) [PH Es] ist wirklich schwer zu sagen, [RE welche Positionen er einnimmt]

(2) Man muß sie also [PH so] behandeln , [RE wie man eine Weltanschauungsbewegung behandelt]

(3) Alles deutet [PH darauf] hin [RE daß sie es nicht schaffen wird]

These examples all have the RE in the *Nachfeld*, but their placement actually has a large variety.

procedure has indeed strong affinity with deep lexical acquisition, except for the fact that in DLA all lexical types are known, and this is not the case in this study: the hand-written lexical type hierarchy is still extended with new types that are derived from the resource treebank, mostly for verbs.

The basic procedure is as follows:

- Traverse the graph top-down.
- For each node:
  - Identify the node's head (or the deepest verb in the verb cluster[3]);
  - For each complement of this node, add this complement to the head's subcategorisation frame.
  - For each modifier, add this head to the possible MOD values of the modifier's head.
- For each lexical item, a mapping of (lemma, morphology) $\rightarrow$ word form is created.

After this procedure, the following information is recorded for the verb lemma 'leisten' from figure 2:

- It has a subcategorisation frame 'npnom-refl-npacc'.
- Its infinitive form is 'leisten'.

The core grammar defines that possible subjects are nominative NPs, expletive 'es' and CPs. Expletives are considered to be entirely syntactic (and not semantic), so they will not receive a dependency relation. Complements may include predicative APs, predicative NPs, genitive, dative and accusative NPs, prepositional complements, CPs, reflexives, separable particles (also purely syntactic), and any combination of these. For non-verbs, the complements are ordered (*i.e.* it is a list, and not a verb). Verb complementation patterns are sets, which means that duplicate complements are not allowed. For verbs, it is also recorded whether the auxiliary verb to mark the perfect tense should be either 'haben' (default) or 'sein' (mostly verbs that have to do with movement). Nouns are annotated with whether they can have appositions or not.

[3]That means that the head of a S/VP-node is assumed to be contained in the lexicon, as it must be some sort of auxiliary.

Results from the derivation procedure are graphed in figure 3. The number of nouns and names is still growing after 45,000 sentences, which is an expected result, given the infinite nature of names and frequent noun compounding. However, it appears that verbs, adjectives and adverbs are converging to a stable level. On the other hand, lexical types are still learnt, and this shows a downside of our approach: the deeper the extraction procedure is, the more data is needed to reach the same level of learning.

The core grammar contains a little less than 100 lexical types, and on top of that, 636 lexical types are learnt, of which 579 are for verbs. It is interesting to see that the number of lexical types is considerably lower than in (Hockenmaier, 2006), where around 2,500 lexical types are learnt. This shows that our approach has a higher level of generalisation, and is presumably a consequence of the fact that the German CCG grammar needs distinct lexical types for verb-initial and verb-final constructions, and for different argument scramblings in the *Mittelfeld*, whereas in our approach, hand-written lexical rules are used to do the scrambling.

The last graph shows that the number of word forms is still insufficient. We assume that each verb can have 28 different word forms. As can be seen, it is clear that only a small part of this area is learnt. One direction for future research might be to find ways to automatically expand the lexicon after the derivation procedure, or to hand-code morphological rules in the core grammar.

4 Parsing

4.1 Methodology

All experiments in this article use the first 45,000 sentences as training data, and the consecutive 5,000 sentences as test data. The remaining 472 sentences are not used. We used the PET parser (Callmeier, 2000) to do all parsing experiments. The parser was instructed to yield a parse error after 50,000 passive edges were used. Ambiguity packing (Oepen and Carroll, 2000) and selective unpacking (Zhang et al., 2007) were used to reduce memory footprint and speed up the selection of the top-1000 analyses. The maximum entropy model, used for selective unpacking, was based on 200 treebanked sentences of up to 20 words from the training set. Part-of-speech tags delivered by the stock version of the TnT tagger (Brants,) were

	Tiger	T.+TnT	GG
Out of vocabulary	71.9 %	5.2 %	55.6 %
Parse error	0.2 %	1.5 %	0.2 %
Unparsed	7.9 %	37.7 %	28.2 %
Parsed	20.0 %	55.6 %	16.0 %
Total	100.0 %	100.0 %	100.0 %
Avg. length	8.6	12.8	8.0
Avg. nr. of parses	399.0	573.1	19.2
Avg. time (s)	9.3	15.8	11.6

Table 1: This table shows coverage results on the held-out test set. The first column denotes how the extracted grammar performs without unknown word guessing. The second column uses PoS tags and generic types to guide the grammar when an unknown word is encountered. The third column is the performance of the fully hand-written HPSG German grammar by (Müller, 2002; Crysmann, 2003). OOV stands for out-of-vocabulary. A parse error is recorded when the passive edge limit (set to 50,000) has been reached. The bottom three rows only gives information about the sentences where the grammar actually returns at least one parse.

	Training set	Test set
All	100.0 %	100.0 %
Avg. length	14.2	13.5
Coverage	79.0 %	69.0 %
Avg. length	13.2	12.8
Correct (top-1000)	52.0%	33.5 %
Avg. length	10.4	8.5

Table 2: Shown are the treebanking results, giving an impression of the quality of the parses. The 'training set' and 'test set' are subsets of 200 sentences from the training and test set, respectively. 'Coverage' means that at least one analysis is found, and 'correct' indicates that the perfect solution was found in the top-1000 parses.

used when unknown word handling was turned on. These tags were connected to generic lexical types by a hand-written mapping. The version of GG that was employed (Müller, 2002; Crysmann, 2003) was dated October 2008[4].

4.2 Results

Table 1 shows coverage figures in three different settings. It is clear that the resulting grammar has a higher coverage than the GG, but this comes at a cost: more ambiguity, and possibly unnecessary ambiguity. Remarkably, the average processing time is lower, even when the sentence lengths and ambiguity rates are higher. We attribute this to the smaller feature structure geometry that is introduced by the core grammar (compared to the GG). Using unknown word handling immediately improved the coverage, by a large margin. Larger ambiguity rates were recorded, and the number of parser errors slightly increased.

Because coverage does not imply quality, we wanted to look at the results in a qualitative fashion. We took a sample of 200 sentences from both the training and the test set, where the ones from the training set did not overlap with the set used to train the MaxEnt model, so that both settings were equally influenced by the rudimentary MaxEnt model. We evaluated for how many sentences the exactly correct parse tree could be found among the top-1000 parses (see table 2). The difference between the performance on the training and test set give an idea of how well the grammar performs on unknown data: if the difference is small, the grammar extends well to unseen data. Compared to evaluating on lexical coverage, we believe this is a more empirical estimation of how close the acquisition process is to convergence.

Based on the kind of parse trees we observed, the impression was that on both sets, performance was reduced due to the limited predictive power of the disambiguation model. There were quite a few sentences for which good parses could be expected, because all lexical entries were present. This experiment also showed that there were systematic ambiguities that were introduced by inconsistent annotation in the Tiger treebank. For in-

[4]It should be noted that little work has gone in to providing unknown word handling mechanisms, and that is why we didn't include it in our results. However, in a CoNLL-2009 shared task paper (Zhang et al., 2009), a coverage of 28.6% was reported when rudimentary methods were used.

stance, the word 'ein' was learnt as both a number (the English 'one') and as an article ('a'), leading to spurious ambiguities for each noun phrase containing the word 'ein', or one of its morphological variants. These two factors reinforced each other: if there is spurious ambiguity, it is even harder for a sparsely trained disambiguation model to pull the correct parse inside the top-1000.

The difference between the two 'correct' numbers in table 2 is rather large, meaning that the 'real' coverage might seem disappointingly low. Not unexpectedly, we found that the generic lexical types for verbs (transitive verb, third person singular) and nouns (any gender, no appositions allowed) was not always correct, harming the results considerably.

A quantitative comparison between deep grammars is always hard. Between DELPH-IN grammars, coverage has been the main method of evaluation. However, this score does not reward richness of the semantic output. Recent evidence from the ERG (Ytrestøl et al., 2009) suggests that the ERG reaches a top-500 coverage of around 70% on an unseen domain, a result that this experiment did not approximate. The goal of GG is not computational, but it serves as a testing ground for linguistic hypotheses. Therefore, the developers have never aimed at high coverage figures, and crafted the GG to give more detailed analyses and to be suited for both parsing and generation. We are happy to observe that the coverage figures in this study are higher than GG's (Zhang et al., 2009), but we realise the limited value of this evaluation method. Future studies will certainly include a more granular evaluation of the grammar's performance.

5 Conclusion and discussion

We showed how a precise, wide-coverage HPSG grammar for German can be created successfully, by constructing a core grammar by hand, and appending it with linguistic information from the Tiger treebank. Although this extracted grammar suffers considerably more from overgeneration than the hand-written GG, we argue that our conservative derivation procedure delivers a more detailed, compact and correct compared to previous deep grammar extraction efforts. The use of the core lexicon allows us to have more linguistically motivated analyses of German than approaches where the core lexicon only comprises the textbook principles/operators. We compared our lexicon extraction results to those from (Hockenmaier, 2006). Also, preliminary parsing experiments are reported, in which we show that this grammar produces reasonable coverage on unseen text.

Although we feel confident about the successful acquisition of the grammar, there still remain some limiting factors in the performance of the grammar when actually parsing. Compared to coverage figures of around 80%, reported by (Riezler et al., 2001), the proportion of parse forests containing the correct parse in this study is rather low. The first limit is the constructional coverage, meaning that the core grammar is not able to construct the correct analysis, even though all lexical entries have been derived correctly before. The most frequent phenomena that are not captured yet are PH/RE constructions and extraposed clauses, and we plan to do an efficient implementation (Crysmann, 2005) of these in a next version of the grammar. Second, as shown in figure 3, data scarcity in the learning of the surface forms of lemmas negatively influences the parser's performance on unseen text.

In this paper, we focused mostly on the correctness of the derivation procedure. We would like to address the real performance of the grammar/parser combination in future work, which can only be done when parses are evaluated according to a more granular method than we have done in this study. Furthermore, we ran into the issue that there is no straightforward way to train larger statistical models automatically, which is due to the fact that our approach does not convert the source treebank to the target formalism's format (in our case HPSG), but instead reads off lexical types and lexical entries directly. We plan to investigate possibilities to have the annotation be guided automatically by the Tiger treebank, so that the disambiguation model can be trained on a much larger amount of training data.

Acknowledgements

We would like to thank Rebecca Dridan, Antske Fokkens, Stephan Oepen and the anonymous reviewers for their valuable contributions to this paper.

References

T. Brants. TnT: a statistical part-of-speech tagger. In *Proceedings of the Sixth Conference on Applied Natural Language Processing*.

S. Brants, S. Dipper, S. Hansen, W. Lezius, and G. Smith. 2002. The TIGER Treebank. In *Proceedings of the Workshop on Treebanks and Linguistic Theories*, pages 24–41.

M. Butt, H. Dyvik, T.H. King, H. Masuichi, and C. Rohrer. 2002. The parallel grammar project. In *International Conference On Computational Linguistics*, pages 1–7.

A. Cahill, M. Burke, R. ODonovan, J. Van Genabith, and A. Way. 2004. Long-distance dependency resolution in automatically acquired wide-coverage PCFG-based LFG approximations. In *Proceedings of ACL-2004*, pages 320–327.

U. Callmeier. 2000. PET–a platform for experimentation with efficient HPSG processing techniques. *Natural Language Engineering*, 6(01):99–107.

B. Carpenter. 1992. *The Logic of Typed Feature Structures: With Applications to Unification Grammars, Logic Programs, and Constraint Resolution*. Cambridge University Press, Cambridge, UK.

E. Charniak and M. Johnson. 2005. Coarse-to-fine n-best parsing and MaxEnt discriminative reranking. In *Proceedings of ACL-2005*, pages 173–180.

A. Copestake, D. Flickinger, C. Pollard, and I. Sag. 2005. Minimal Recursion Semantics: An Introduction. *Research on Language & Computation*, 3(4):281–332.

A. Copestake. 2002. *Implementing Typed Feature Structure Grammars*. CSLI Publications, Stanford, CA, USA.

B. Crysmann. 2003. On the efficient implementation of German verb placement in HPSG. In *Proceedings of RANLP-2003*, pages 112–116.

B. Crysmann. 2005. Relative Clause Extraposition in German: An Efficient and Portable Implementation. *Research on Language & Computation*, 3(1):61–82.

A. Dubey and F. Keller. 2003. Probabilistic parsing for German using sister-head dependencies. In *Proceedings of the 41st Annual Meeting on Association for Computational Linguistics*, pages 96–103.

D. Flickinger. 2000. On building a more effcient grammar by exploiting types. *Natural Language Engineering*, 6(1):15–28.

J. Hockenmaier and M. Steedman. 2002. Acquiring compact lexicalized grammars from a cleaner treebank. In *Proceedings of LREC-2002*, pages 1974–1981.

J. Hockenmaier. 2006. Creating a CCGbank and a Wide-Coverage CCG Lexicon for German. In *Proceedings of ACL-2006*, pages 505–512.

A.K. Joshi and Y. Schabes. 1997. Tree-adjoining grammars. *Handbook of formal languages*, 3:69–124.

R.M. Kaplan and J. Bresnan. 1995. Lexical-Functional Grammar: A formal system for grammatical representation. *Formal Issues in Lexical-Functional Grammar*, pages 29–130.

T. Kiss and B. Wesche. 1991. Verb order and head movement. *Text Understanding in LILOG, Lecture Notes in Artificial Intelligence*, 546:216–242.

D. Magerman. 1995. Statistical decision-tree models for parsing. In *Proceedings of ACL-1995*, pages 276–283.

Y. Miyao, T. Ninomiya, and J. Tsujii. 2004. Corpus-oriented grammar development for acquiring a Head-driven Phrase Structure Grammar from the Penn Treebank. In *Proceedings of IJCNLP-2004*.

S. Müller. 2002. *Complex Predicates: Verbal Complexes, Resultative Constructions, and Particle Verbs in German*. CSLI Publications, Stanford, CA, USA.

S. Oepen and J. Carroll. 2000. Ambiguity packing in constraint-based parsing: practical results. In *Proceedings of NAACL-2000*, pages 162–169.

C.J. Pollard and I.A. Sag. 1994. *Head-Driven Phrase Structure Grammar*. University Of Chicago Press, Chicago, IL, USA.

S. Riezler, T.H. King, R.M. Kaplan, R. Crouch, J.T. Maxwell III, and M. Johnson. 2001. Parsing the Wall Street Journal using a Lexical-Functional Grammar and discriminative estimation techniques. In *Proceedings of ACL-2001*, pages 271–278.

M. Steedman. 1996. *Surface structure and interpretation*. MIT Press, Cambridge, MA, USA.

G. Ytrestøl, D. Flickinger, and S. Oepen. 2009. Extracting and Annotating Wikipedia Sub-Domains. In *Proceedings of the Seventh International Workshop on Treebanks and Linguistic Theories*, pages 185–197.

Y. Zhang, S. Oepen, and J. Carroll. 2007. Efficiency in Unification-Based N-Best Parsing. In *Proceedings of the Tenth International Conference on Parsing Technologies*, pages 48–59.

Y. Zhang, R. Wang, and S.. Oepen. 2009. Hybrid Multilingual Parsing with HPSG for SRL. In *Proceedings of CoNLL-2009, to appear*.

Parenthetical Constructions - an Argument against Modularity

Eva Banik
The Open University
Milton Keynes, UK
e.banik@open.ac.uk

Abstract

This paper presents an argument against modularizing linguistic information in natural language generation systems. We argue that complex linguistic constructions require grammatical information to be located in the same module, in order to avoid over-complicating the system architecture. We demonstrate this point by showing how parenthetical constructions — which have only been generated in previous systems using an aggregation or revision module — can be generated by a surface realizer when using an integrated grammar.

1 Introduction

The ultimate aim of research on natural language generation is to develop large-scale, domain independent NLG systems, which are able to generate high quality, fluent and well-formatted texts. Ideally the produced texts will be as long as needed to convey the information given in the input and should be presented in a style that is appropriate for the purposes of the user. Current NLG systems typically produce paragraph-length text tailored to a specific domain and the grammars in these systems contain only a limited number of grammatical constructions, typically collected during a corpus study of example documents. Often the grammar is implemented using schemas or "canned" expressions, and individual grammatical levels are distributed in independent modules.

Organizing the grammar this way severely limits the flexibility of NLG systems. It has long been recognized in the literature that text fluency can be improved by modeling interactions between grammar modules. The most commonly mentioned interactions are those among discourse/rhetorical relations and syntax (Scott and Souza, 1990; Hovy, 1993; Callaway, 2003), rhetorical relations, syntax and referring expressions (Kibble and Power, 2004); and layout and referring expressions (N. Bouayad-Agha, 2001). It is clear that in order to generate high quality, coherent discourse, a generator needs access to a grammar which is able to model the interdependent, context-sensitive behaviour of these separate linguistic phenomena.

In this paper we draw a parallel between grammar design and the design of natural language generation systems. We argue that in order to generate complex linguistic constructions, current NLG systems tend to have overly complicated architectures. To illustrate this point we show how a surface realizer can take on tasks from other components when linguistic information from different grammar modules (and hence, system modules) is integrated. This simplifies system architecture by reducing the need for interaction between modules and enables the generator to produce more complex and coherent text. We illustrate this point by first showing constraints that parenthetical constructions impose on pronominalization. Then we present a grammar which integrates a representation for referring expressions into a syntax/discourse grammar. Finally we show that using this grammar, we can generate complex, coherent paragraphs which contain parenthetical constructions using only a surface realizer.

2 The problem of generating parenthetical constructions

Parentheticals are constructions that provide less important or background information in texts and they are a prime example of interactions between referring expressions, syntax, layout and discourse structure. Parentheticals help readers distinguish between more and less important propositions and therefore significantly increase the fluency and readability of the generated text. Despite this ma-

Proceedings of the 2009 Workshop on Grammar Engineering Across Frameworks, ACL-IJCNLP 2009, pages 46–53,
Suntec, Singapore, 6 August 2009.

jor effect on the quality of the generated text, current natural language generation systems still do not have a principled way of producing parentheticals. In this paper we focus on parenthetical constructions which take the form of a subordinate clause introduced by a discourse connective. Some examples of this type of parentheticals in the Wall Street Journal are illustrated (1):

(1) a The irony is that the attack commercial, *after getting a boost in last year's presidential campaign,* has come of age in an off-off election year with only a few contests scattered across the country.

b the 1989 fall total of 80, *while well below 1988 activity,* shows a steady ratcheting up in citizen referenda and initiatives

c pollination, *while easy in corn because the carrier is wind,* is more complex and involves insects as carriers in crops such as cotton

The examples in (2) illustrate the difficulties in generating parenthetical constructions by showing some possible but *incoherent* realizations of the same message. In particular, they illustrate the importance of appropriate punctuation marks (2a), syntactic requirements of discourse connectives (2b), the limit on embedding (2c), and the importance of ordering syntactic arguments (thematic structure/information structure) (2d).

(2) a # The FDA though it bans Elixir since it contains Gestodene approves Elixir Plus.

b # The FDA – but it bans Elixir since it contains Gestodene – approves Elixir Plus.

c # The FDA though since Elixir contains Gestodene , it bans Elixir approves Elixir Plus.

d # The FDA, since Gestodene is an ingredient of Elixir, bans Elixir. But it approves Elixir Plus.

Correct realizations of the same message would include:

(3) a The FDA — though it bans Elixir since it contains Gestodene — approves Elixir Plus .

b The FDA bans Elixir because it contains Gestodene. However, Elixir Plus is approved by the FDA

c The FDA approves Elixir Plus although Elixir — since it contains Gestodene — is banned by the FDA.

Generation systems that produce output similar to the examples in (3) have three kinds of strategies: either a text planning module chooses a discourse connective and decides the position and ordering of clauses (Hovy, 1993) or aggregation is considered to be one of the tasks of the sentence planning module (Shaw, 2002); or a revision module performs aggregation opportunistically (Robin, 1994; Callaway and Lester, 1997). However, none of these systems handle parenthetical constructions in a principled way. Systems where aggregation is part of the text planning module only produce complex sentences made up of clauses joined by discourse connectives – sentence-medial subordinate clauses are not generated at all. In revision-based systems, the output often needs to be corrected after aggregation. For example, Robin's system includes various transformations to correct redundancies, ambiguities or invalid lexical collocations introduced by the revision module. In Shaw's system, the referring expression generation module is run twice, once before and once after aggregation. In general, the ordering of aggregation rules and the interactions between them pose further problems where aggregation is separated into an independent module.We propose a different approach to modeling interactions between linguistic information in separate grammar modules. We argue that constraints that are at the interface of modules (syntactic constraints on referring expressions, discourse-level constraints on syntax, constraints imposed by layout on discourse, etc.) should be stored in an integrated grammar, and only straightforward decisions — which do not require information from a separate grammatical level — should be separated out into individual modules.

As an example, we show a grammar which is capable of generating parenthetical constructions in a principled way. The grammar includes

- a representation for discourse connectives and discourse-level constraints they impose on syntax;
- referring expressions and syntactic constraints on them;

- elements of layout (punctuation marks for main clauses and parentheticals).

We show that by incorporating the above kinds of linguistic information into the grammar of a surface realizer we can improve the flexibility of the system (i.e., generate more paraphrases for the same input) and improve the quality of the generated text without adding more modules to the system.

2.1 Syntactic constraints on pronominalization

To design a grammar for parenthetical constructions, we have carried out a corpus study on embedded rhetorical relations in the RST treebank (Banik and Lee, 2008). The corpus study has shown that the most numerous class of embedded subordinate clauses that occur in sentence-medial position contain a subject pronoun (as in 4a). This embedded subject pronoun in all cases referred back to the subject of the matrix clause, which always immediately preceded the subordinate clause. The pronoun can be either explicit (as in 4a) or implicit (as in the examples in 1). Of the 119 sentence-medial subordinate clauses that we looked at in the study, 35 were of this type (what we call pseudo-relatives).[1] This suggests that in sentence-medial subordinate clauses (or sentence-final ones immediately following the main clause object) the type of a referring expression is solely determined by syntax, much like a WH-pronoun in relative clauses.

(4) a Elixir, since it contains Gestodene, is banned by the FDA.

b # Elixir, since Elixir contains Gestodene, is banned by the FDA.

c # It, since Elixir contains Gestodene, is banned by the FDA.

d # The FDA, since it contains Gestodene, banned Elixir.

The constraints on the form of referring expressions selected for the matrix clause and subordinate clause subjects in these cases can be stated as follows:

[1]Of the rest, 30 were 'free' subordinate clauses (subordinate clauses that are equally felicitous in sentence-initial or sentence final positions, typically they do not contain any pronouns). The rest of the cases were either time adverbials (20) or scopal elements (22).

- the subject of the subordinate clause has to be realized as a pronoun. (c.f. 4b)
- the subject of the main clause cannot be a pronoun (c.f. 4c)
- the subject pronoun in the subordinate clause will be resolved as referring to an entity mentioned in the matrix clause; this entity has to precede the subordinate clause (c.f. 4d)

In addition to modeling the above constraints, in order to generate parentheticals a generation system also has to

- insert the appropriate discourse connective for the subordinate clause (c.f.2b) and
- insert appropriate punctuation marks on either side of the subordinate clause to avoid potential garden path effects.

3 An integrated discourse-syntax grammar

In order to generate coherent discourse, a generation system needs access to a grammar that is capable of representing multisentential text. In modular systems this is typically achieved by two modules: a text planning module which constructs a text plan and a surface realizer that converts the text plan into sentences. However, text planning and linguistic realization are not two independent processes and many linguistic decisions are in fact made by the text planner. The interactions between text planning and linguistic realization in modular systems have been handled in several ways, including backtracking (Appelt, 1985), interleaving the two components (McDonald, 1983) and restrictive planning (Hovy, 1988). These approaches however make the system inflexible because all possible interactions between modules have to be anticipated by the system designer.

Another, more recent approach to tackle this problem is to use lexicalization not only for sentences but also for texts. The theoretical background for lexicalization on the discourse level has been laid down for Tree Adjoining Grammar (Joshi and Schabes, 1997) by several researchers, including Webber (2004), and Danlos (2000). In particular, Danlos (2000) shows that extending lexicalization to the discourse level makes it possible to completely integrate text planning and surface realization.

We have designed a Tree Adjoining Grammar for parenthetical constructions following this latter approach. Elementary trees in the grammar are associated with a flat semantic representation. The trees integrate syntax and discourse representations in the sense that each sentence-level elementary tree includes one or more discourse-level nodes. The elementary trees in Fig. 1 illustrate what we mean by this: every lexical item that would normally project a sentence in a syntactic grammar (i.e., an S-rooted tree) here projects a discourse clause (i.e., a Dc rooted tree). Every predicate that projects a discourse clause is assigned two kinds of elementary trees: a discourse initial tree (e.g., Fig. 1a) and a discourse continuing tree (e.g., Fig. 1b), which takes the preceding discourse clause as an argument.

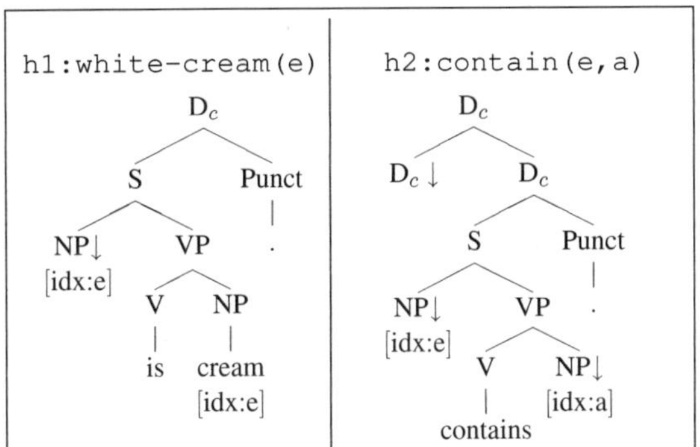

(a) discourse initial

(b) discourse continuing

Figure 1: Elementary syntax/discourse trees

The combination of these two trees corresponds to the empty connective ($\oplus$ in Danlos (2000)). Other types of discourse connectives are implemented in the grammar the usual way (see e.g. Danlos (2000)).

4 Referring expressions

One of the challenges of generating paraphrases from a semantic representation is that in some versions there will be a mismatch between the number of noun phrases needed to make the output syntactically well-formed and the number of semantic arguments in the input which can potentially become a noun phrase.

This happens whenever a discourse entity is the argument of more than one semantic predicate. For example, (5) shows possible realizations of the following input where (5a) contains three syntactic slots for "Elixir", (5b,c) contain two slots, and (5d) only one:

```
h0:white-cream(e)
h1:contains(e,g)
h2:elixir(e)
h3:gestodene(g)
h4:ban(f,e)
h5:fda(f)
```

(5) a Elixir is a white cream. Elixir contains gestodene. Elixir is banned by the FDA.
  b This white cream, Elixir, contains gestodene. It is banned by the FDA.
  c Elixir is a white cream, which contains gestodene. It is banned by the FDA.
  d Elixir, a white cream banned by the FDA, contains gestodene.

The task of a generation system is to decide what predicate-argument structure to choose and to decide how the individual noun phrases should be represented. In most systems creating the syntactic "slots" is the task of a text planning or sentence planning module, and filling them in with the right noun phrases is the task of a referring expression generation module, i.e., the referring expression module decides whether an NP slot should be realized as a name, a pronoun or a description.

This division of labour makes it difficult to represent syntactic constraints on pronominalization exhibited by the examples in the previous section, where pronouns are either prohibited or obligatory in specific syntactic contexts.

To model these constraints we include a representation for underspecified referring expressions in the grammar by replacing NP substitution nodes with a referring expression leaf node as illustrated in Fig.2. This allows syntactic constraints to be 'posted' on referring expressions in the appropriate contexts while completely specifying the form of the underspecified slots still remains the task of a referring expression module. In other words, we factor out pronominalization decisions dictated by syntax from pronominalization decisions dictated by discourse level constraints.

Treating pronouns in subordinate clauses differently from pronouns in main clauses has independent justification from psycholinguistics and theoretical linguistics. For example, Miltsakaki (2003) has carried out psycholinguistic experiments on complex sentences containing relative clauses. The experiments show that pronouns in embedded clauses tend to refer back to an entity

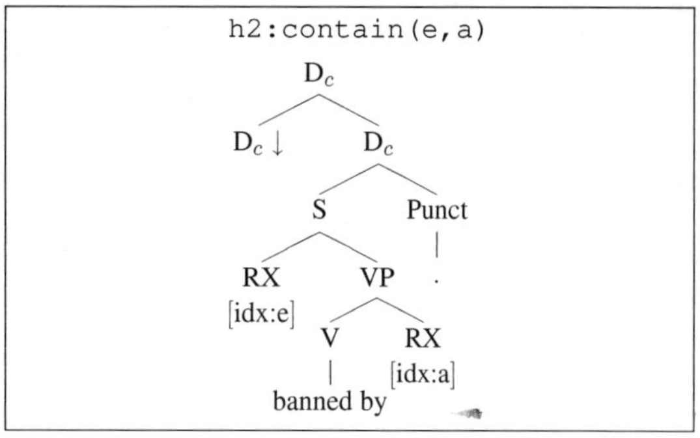

Figure 2: Elementary trees with referring expressions

in the matrix clause, whereas referring expressions in main clauses tend to find their antecedent in the previous main clause. This suggests that pronominalization should be treated differently in subordinate clauses than in main clauses. Research in theoretical linguistics underlines this claim, where Kehler (2002) has shown that apparent discrepancies between different accounts of pronominalization can be reconciled if each method is applied in a different discourse context.

To sum up, in this integrated approach part of the job of the referring expression generation module is taken over by the grammar, namely

- pronominalization of discourse entities in subordinate clauses and
- decisions about when *not* to realize underspecified referring expressions as pronouns.

5 Representing parenthetical constructions

Integrating referring expressions into the grammar this way makes it possible to state syntactic constraints on pronominalization.

5.1 Pronoun prohibited

(6) a Elixir, an illegal drug, is banned by the FDA.

b # It, an illegal drug, is banned by the FDA.

The constraint that parenthetical constructions such as appositives, relative clauses or parenthetical subordinate clauses cannot follow a pronoun is illustrated by the contrast in (6). Using the elementary trees described in the previous section this constraint can now be stated by adding a feature (`[pron:no]`) to the foot node of auxiliary trees, as illustrated in Fig. 3. When the auxiliary tree is adjoined onto an NP, the feature is percolated to the underspecified referring expression node, which will block the referring expression module from realizing this noun phrase as a pronoun.

5.2 Pronoun obligatory

(7) a Elixir, since it contains Gestodene, is banned by the FDA.

b # Elixir, since Elixir contains Gestodene, is banned by the FDA.

Another case where syntax imposes constraints on pronominalization is contexts where pronouns are not allowed, as illustrated by the example in (7). The discourse connective 'since' is assigned an NP auxiliary tree in this context, which takes the embedded clause as an argument. The features on the auxiliary tree state that the subject of this embedded clause should be expressed by a pronoun and that it should refer to the same discourse entity as the head noun that the auxiliary tree adjoins to. When the discourse connective is combined with the embedded clause, these features are percolated to the referring expression in subject position, requiring it to be realized by a pronoun. Figure 4 illustrates the elementary trees and the derived tree for the embedded clause in (7).

6 Comparison

As an experiment, we have implemented a grammar fragment in the GenI surface realizer (Kow, 2007) and regenerated an example from the ICONOCLAST generator (Power et al., 2003). The example we used is represented by the following input semantics:

```
h1:   elixir(e)
h2:   fda(f)
h3:   elixir_plus(p)
h4:   gestodene(g)
h5:   contain(e g)
h6:   ban(f e)
h7:   approve(f p)
h8:   concession(h6 h7)
h9:   cause(h5 h6)
h10:  contain(p o)
h11:  oestradiol(o)
h12:  cause(h10 h7)
```

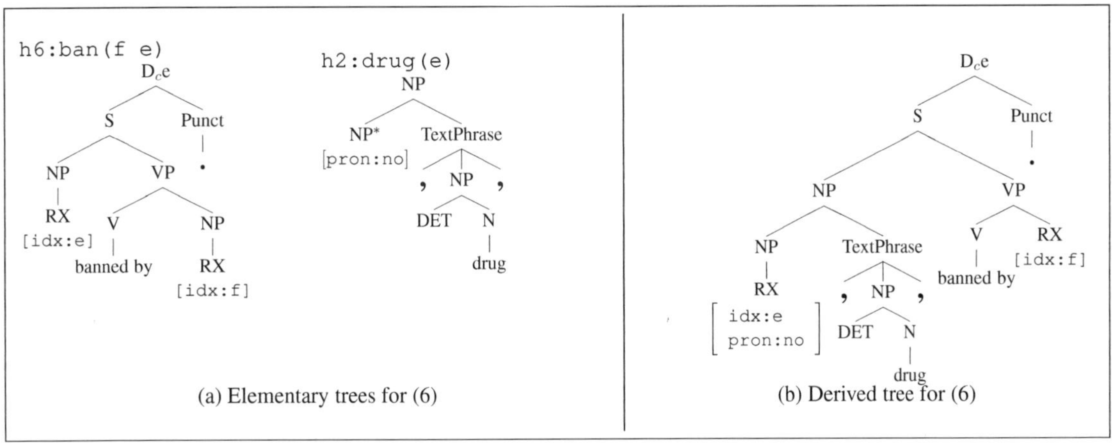

Figure 3: Pronouns not allowed before an appositive

(a) Elementary trees for (6)

(b) Derived tree for (6)

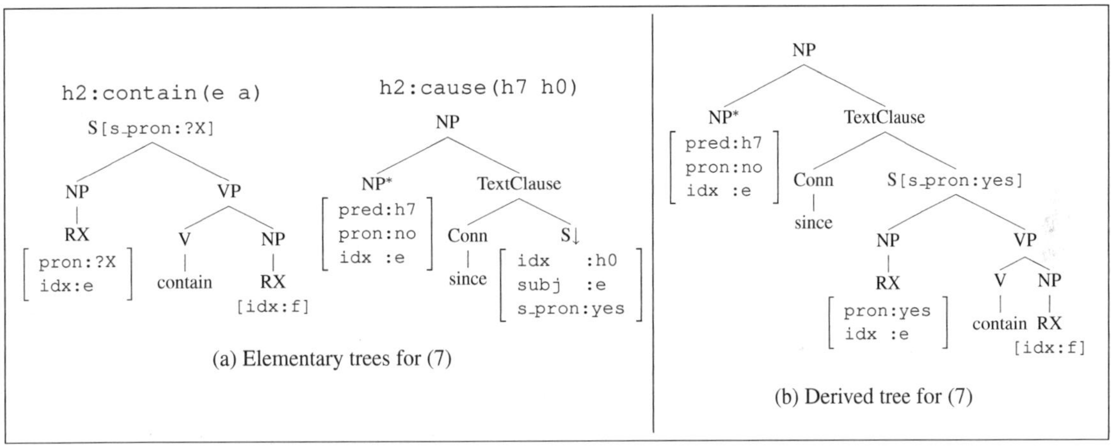

Figure 4: Obligatory pronouns in parenthetical subordinate clauses

(a) Elementary trees for (7)

(b) Derived tree for (7)

ICONOCLAST is a constraint-based system which integrates text planning, document planning and pronominalization to generate all possible paraphrases for a given input. It uses a version of Centering Theory (Grosz et al., 1995) adapted to natural language generation to decide when to pronominalize noun phrases in the generated text. ICONOCLAST has an overgenerate and test approach, where all possible paraphrases are generated and the solutions are ranked according to a set of soft constraints. The system generated 172 solutions for the above input, of which (8) illustrates the top three:

(8)
a Since Elixir contains gestodene it is banned by the FDA. However, the FDA approves Elixir Plus since Elixir Plus contains oestradiol.

b Elixir contains gestodene so it is banned by the FDA. However, the FDA approves ElixirPlus since ElixirPlus contains oestradiol.

c Elixir is banned by the FDA since it contains gestodene. However, ElixirPlus is approved by the FDA since it contains oestradiol.

We have regenerated the same text, using only a surface realizer and the grammar described in the previous sections, without a referring expression generation module. A post-processing script transforms RX nodes into a pronoun when they have the relevant feature ([pron:yes]) and into a name when the [pron] feature is missing or its value is no. The surface realizer produced 208 solutions for the same input, of which 96 contained parentheticals. Some of the output is illustrated in (9). Since sentence final parenthetical constructions are impossible to distinguish from sentence-final subordinate clauses in many cases, there is an overlap between the solutions generated by ICONOCLAST and the 96 solutions generated by our

(9) a The FDA bans Elixir since Elixir contains gestodene. However, Elixir Plus (since it contains oestradiol) is approved by the FDA.

b Since Elixir Plus contains oestradiol, although the FDA bans Elixir (since it contains gestodene), Elixir Plus is approved by the FDA.

c Elixir contains gestodene. Consequently, Elixir is banned by the FDA. However, Elixir Plus (since it contains oestradiol) is approved by the FDA.

d Elixir Plus contains oestradiol. Consequently, although the FDA bans Elixir (since it contains gestodene), the FDA approves Elixir Plus.

e Elixir Plus (since it contains oestradiol) is approved by the FDA (although it bans Elixir since it contains gestodene).

f The FDA bans Elixir (since it contains gestodene). However, Elixir Plus is approved by the FDA since Elixir Plus contains oestradiol.

grammar which contain parentheticals. Also, despite the fact that the two systems use the same discourse connectives and a very similar grammar, there are slight differences in the constructions produced. For example, ICONOCLAST allows subordinating conjunctions to "dominate" coordinating conjunctions, producing solutions like the one in (10), although these solutions are assigned at least 4 defects in all cases. These constructions are not allowed in our grammar.

(10) Although Elixir contains gestodene so it is banned by the FDA ElixirPlus contains oestradiol so it is approved by the FDA.

Though comparing the generated solutions is not a straightforward task because of these subtle differences and the sheer number of the solutions produced, the two systems do generate a number of very similar outputs, including the ones shown in (8). However, a significant difference is that our system generates coherent texts which include parenthetical constructions, and which are not generated by ICONOCLAST at all.

7 Related work

Our grammar design was inspired by three discourse-level extensions of Lexicalized Tree Adjoining Grammar. A common idea behind all these approaches is to build an integrated text understanding or generation system in which the same mechanisms are used for the sentence and discourse levels.

DLTAG (Webber, 2004) is an extension of LTAG in which discourse syntax is projected by different types of discourse connectives. In this approach discourse-level syntax is considered to be a separate layer on top of sentence-level syntax and there are two kinds of discourse connectives: anaphoric and structural (Webber et al., 2003). This analysis is not suitable for natural language generation systems which need to have an explicit representation for the arguments of discourse connectives.

G-TAG (Danlos, 2000) is another discourse-level extension of TAG where underspecified 'g-derivation trees' are created for a conceptual input and grouped into lexical databases. A g-derivation tree specifies a set of surface variants, one of which is produced by linearization of the g-derived tree. The other surface variants are created by a post-processing module. While this methodology efficiently reduces the search space of solutions by grouping them together, it assumes that all variants of the same sentence can be generated in the same discourse context.

Most recently, Danlos (2008) introduces D-STAG, a discourse level synchronous TAG coupled with Segmented Discourse Representation Theory (Asher, 1993). In this framework the sentential grammar (S-TAG) and the discourse grammar (D-STAG) are not integrated, therefore discourses where arguments of discourse relations come from discontinuous text spans (as in relative clauses or other types of parentheticals) are not handled by the theory.

8 Conclusions

We have presented an argument against modularizing linguistic information in natural language generation systems. We have argued that complex linguistic constructions which require interactions between several system components are best represented in natural language generation systems using an integrated grammar. As an example, we have presented the problem of generating parenthetical constructions. Current natural language generation systems either do not generate these constructions at all, or if they do, they do not have a principled approach to the problem and generate parentheticals by adding more modules to a pipeline. We have shown that parentheticals can be generated in a principled way using a surface realizer, when it is equipped with an integrated grammar which incorporates information about syntax, discourse and referring expressions. The solutions produced by our surface realizer demonstrate that this approach enhances the fluency of the generated text and the flexibility of generation systems, without adding extra components or changing the system's architecture.

References

D.E. Appelt. 1985. *Planning English sentences*. Cambridge University Press, Cambridge.

N. Asher. 1993. *Reference to Abstract Objects in English*. Kluwer, Dordrecht.

E. Banik and A. Lee. 2008. A study of parentheticals in discourse corpora – implications for NLG systems. In *Proceedings of LREC 2008, Marrakesh*.

C. B. Callaway and J. C. Lester. 1997. Dynamically improving explanations: A revision-based approach to explanation generation. In *Fifteenth International Joint Conference on Artificial Intelligence*, pages 952–58, Nagoya, Japan.

C. B. Callaway. 2003. Integrating discourse markers into a pipelined natural language generation architecture. In *ACL '03: Proceedings of the 41st Annual Meeting on Association for Computational Linguistics*, pages 264–271.

L. Danlos. 2000. G-TAG: A lexicalized formalism for text generation inspired by Tree Adjoining Grammar. In A. Abeille and O. Rambow, editors, *Tree Adjoining Grammars: Formalisms, linguistic analysis and processing*, pages 343–370. CSLI, Stanford.

L. Danlos. 2008. D-STAG: Parsing discourse with synchronous TAG and SDRT background. In *Proceedings of the Third International Workshop on Constraints in Discourse (CID'2008) Postdam*.

B.J. Grosz, A.K. Joshi, and S Weinstein. 1995. Centering: a framework for modelling the local coherence of discourse. *Computational Linguistics*, 21(2):203–225.

E. H. Hovy. 1988. Two types of planning in language generation. In *Proceedings of the 26th annual meeting on Association for Computational Linguistics*, pages 179–186, Morristown, NJ, USA. Association for Computational Linguistics.

Eduard H. Hovy. 1993. Automated discourse generation using discourse structure relations. *Artificial Intelligence*, 63(1-2):341–385.

A. K. Joshi and Y. Schabes. 1997. Tree-Adjoining Grammars. In Rosenberg and Salomaa, editors, *Handbook of Formal Languages and Automata*, volume 3, pages 69–124. Springer-Verlag, Heidelberg.

A. Kehler. 2002. *Coherence, Reference and the Theory of Grammar*. CSLI.

R. Kibble and R. Power. 2004. Optimizing referential coherence in text generation. *Computational Linguistics*, 30(4):401–416.

E. Kow. 2007. *Surface realisation: ambiguity and determinism*. Ph.D. thesis, Universite de Henri Poincare.

D. D. McDonald. 1983. Natural language generation as a computational problem. In M. Brady and Robert Berwick, editors, *Computational Models of Discourse*, pages 209–265. MIT Press.

E. Miltsakaki. 2003. *The Syntax-Discourse Interface: Effects of the Main-Subordinate Distinction on Attention Structure*. Ph.D. thesis, Department of Linguistics, University of Pennsylvania.

R. Power N. Bouayad-Agha, D. Scott. 2001. The influence of layout on the interpretation of referring expressions. In L. Degand Y. Bestgen W. Spooren L. van Waes, editor, *Multidisciplinary Approaches to Discourse*, pages 133–141.

R. Power, D. Scott, and N. Bouayad-Agha. 2003. Document structure. *Computational Linguistics*, 29(4):211–260.

J. Robin. 1994. *Revision-based generation of Natural Language Summaries providing historical Background*. Ph.D. thesis, Columbia University.

D. Scott and C. S. Souza. 1990. Getting the message across in RST-based text generation. In C. Mellish R. Dale M. Zock, editor, *Current Research in Natural Language Generation*, pages 31–56. Academic Press.

J. Shaw. 2002. *Clause Aggregation: An approach to generating concise text*. Ph.D. thesis, Columbia University.

B. Webber, M. Stone, A. Joshi, and A. Knott. 2003. Anaphora and discourse structure. *Computational Linguistics*, 29(4):545–587.

B. Webber. 2004. D-LTAG: extending lexicalized TAG to discourse. *Cognitive Science*, 28(5):751–779.

Using Artificially Generated Data to Evaluate Statistical Machine Translation

Manny Rayner, Paula Estrella, Pierrette Bouillon
University of Geneva, TIM/ISSCO
40 bvd du Pont-d'Arve, CH-1211 Geneva 4, Switzerland
{Emmanuel.Rayner,Paula.Estrella,Pierrette.Bouillon}@unige.ch

Beth Ann Hockey
Mail Stop 19-26, UCSC UARC
NASA Ames Research Center, Moffett Field, CA 94035–1000
bahockey@ucsc.edu

Yukie Nakao
LINA, Nantes University, 2, rue de la Houssinière, BP 92208 44322 Nantes Cedex 03
yukie.nakao@univ-nantes.fr

Abstract

Although Statistical Machine Translation (SMT) is now the dominant paradigm within Machine Translation, we argue that it is far from clear that it can outperform Rule-Based Machine Translation (RBMT) on small- to medium-vocabulary applications where high precision is more important than recall. A particularly important practical example is medical speech translation. We report the results of experiments where we configured the various grammars and rule-sets in an Open Source medium-vocabulary multi-lingual medical speech translation system to generate large aligned bilingual corpora for English $\rightarrow$ French and English $\rightarrow$ Japanese, which were then used to train SMT models based on the common combination of Giza++, Moses and SRILM. The resulting SMTs were unable fully to reproduce the performance of the RBMT, with performance topping out, even for English $\rightarrow$ French, with less than 70% of the SMT translations of previously unseen sentences agreeing with RBMT translations. When the outputs of the two systems differed, human judges reported the SMT result as frequently being worse than the RBMT result, and hardly ever better; moreover, the added robustness of the SMT only yielded a small improvement in recall, with a large penalty in precision.

1 Introduction

When Statistical Machine Translation (SMT) was first introduced in the early 90s, it encountered a hostile reception, and many people in the research community were unwilling to believe it could ever be a serious competitor to symbolic approaches (cf. for example (Arnold et al., 1994)). The pendulum has now swung all the way to the other end of the scale; right now, the prevailing wisdom within the research community is that SMT is the only truly viable architecture, and that rule-based machine translation (RBMT) is ultimately doomed to failure. In this paper, one of our initial concerns will be to argue for a compromise position. In our opinion, the initial scepticism about SMT was not groundless; the arguments presented against it often took the form of examples involving deep linguistic reasoning, which, it was claimed, would be hard to address using surface methods. Proponents of RBMT had, however, greatly underestimated the extent to which SMT would be able to tackle the problem of robustness, where it appears to be far more powerful than RBMT. For most machine translation applications, robustness is the central issue, so SMT's current preeminence is hardly surprising.

Even for the large-vocabulary tasks where SMT does best, the situation is by no means as clear as one might imagine: according to (Wilks, 2007), purely statistical systems are still unable to outperform SYSTRAN. In this paper, we will however be more concerned with limited-domain MT tasks, where robustness is not the key requirement, and accuracy is paramount. An immediate exam-

Proceedings of the 2009 Workshop on Grammar Engineering Across Frameworks, ACL-IJCNLP 2009, pages 54–62,
Suntec, Singapore, 6 August 2009.

ple is medical speech translation, which is establishing itself as an an application area of some significance (Bouillon et al., 2006; Bouillon et al., 2008a). Translation in medical applications needs to be extremely accurate, since mistranslations can have serious or even fatal consequences. At the panel discussion at the 2008 COLING workshop on safety-critical speech translation (Rayner et al., 2008), the consensus opinion, based on input from practising physicians, was that an appropriate evaluation metric for medical applications would be heavily slanted towards accuracy, as opposed to robustness. If the metric is normalised so as to award 0 points for no translation, and 1 point for a correct translation, the estimate was that a suitable score for an incorrect translation would be something between –25 and –100 points. With these requirements, it seems unlikely that a robust, broad-coverage architecture has much chance of success. The obvious strategy is to build a limited-domain controlled-language system, and tune it to the point where accuracy reaches the desired level.

For systems of this kind, it is at least *conceivable* that RBMT may be able to outperform SMT. The next question is how to investigate the issues in a methodologically even-handed way. A few studies, notably (Seneff et al., 2006), suggest that rule-based translation may in fact be preferable in these cases. (Another related experiment is described in (Dugast et al., 2008), though this was carried out in a large-vocabulary system). These studies, however, have not been widely cited. One possible explanation is suspicion about methodological issues. Seneff and her colleagues trained their SMT system on 20 000 sentence pairs, a small number by the standards of SMT. It is *a priori* not implausible that more training data would have enabled them to create an SMT system that was as good as, or better than, the rule-based system.

In this paper, our primary goal is to take this kind of objection seriously, and develop a methodology designed to enable a tight comparison between rule-based and statistical architectures. In particular, we wish to examine the widely believed claim that SMT is now inherently better than RBMT. In order to do this, we start with a limited-domain RBMT system; we use it to automatically generate a large corpus of aligned pairs, which is used to train a corresponding SMT system. We then compare the performance of the two systems.

Our argument will be that this situation essentially represents an upper bound for what is possible using the SMT approach in a limited domain. It has been widely remarked that quality, as well as quantity, of training data is important for good SMT; in many projects, significant effort is expended to clean the original training data. Here, since the data is automatically generated by a rule-based system, we can be sure that it is already completely clean (in the sense of being internally consistent), and we can generate as large a quantity of it as we require. The application, moreover, uses only a smallish vocabulary and a fairly constrained syntax. If the derived SMT system is unable to match the original RBMT system's performance, it seems reasonable to claim that this shows that there are types of applications where RBMT architectures are superior.

The experiments described have been carried out using MedSLT, an Open Source interlingua-based limited-domain medical speech translation system. The rest of the paper is organised as follows. Section 2 provides background on the MedSLT system. Section 3 describes the experimental framework, and Section 4 the results obtained. Section 5 concludes.

2 The MedSLT System

MedSLT (Bouillon et al., 2005; Bouillon et al., 2008b) is a medium-vocabulary interlingua-based Open Source speech translation system for doctor-patient medical examination questions, which provides any-language-to-any-language translation capabilities for all languages in the set English, French, Japanese, Arabic, Catalan. Both speech recognition and translation are rule-based. Speech recognition runs on the Nuance 8.5 recognition platform, with grammar-based language models built using the Open Source Regulus compiler. As described in (Rayner et al., 2006), each domain-specific language model is extracted from a general resource grammar using corpus-based methods driven by a seed corpus of domain-specific examples. The seed corpus, which typically contains between 500 and 1500 utterances, is then used a second time to add probabilistic weights to the grammar rules; this substantially improves recognition performance (Rayner et al., 2006, §11.5). Vocabulary sizes and performance measures for speech recognition in the three languages where serious evaluations have been carried out are shown in Figure 1.

Language	Vocab	WER	SemER
English	447	6%	11%
French	1025	8%	10%
Japanese	422	3%	4%

Table 1: Recognition performance for English, French and Japanese MedSLT recognisers. "Vocab" = number of surface words in source language recogniser vocabulary; "WER" = Word Error Rate for source language recogniser, on in-coverage material; "SemER" = semantic error rate (proportion of utterances failing to produce correct interlingua) for source language recogniser, on in-coverage material.

At run-time, the recogniser produces a source-langage semantic representation. This is first translated by one set of rules into an interlingual form, and then by a second set into a target language representation. A target-language Regulus grammar, compiled into generation form, turns this into one or more possible surface strings, after which a set of generation preferences picks one out. Finally, the selected string is realised in spoken form. Robustness issues are addressed by means of a back-up statistical recogniser, which drives a robust embedded help system. The purpose of the help system (Chatzichrisafis et al., 2006) is to guide the user towards supported coverage; it performs approximate matching of output from the statistical recogniser again a library of sentences which have been marked as correctly processed during system development, and then presents the closest matches to the user.

Examples of typical English domain sentences and their translations into French and Japanese are shown in Figure 2.

3 Experimental framework

In the literature on language modelling, there is a known technique for bootstrapping a statistical language model (SLM) from a grammar-based language model (GLM). The grammar which forms the basis of the GLM is sampled randomly in order to create an arbitrarily large corpus of examples; these examples are then used as a training corpus to build the SLM (Jurafsky et al., 1995; Jonson, 2005). We adapt this process in a straightforward way to construct an SMT for a given language pair, using the source language grammar, the source-to-interlingua translation rules, the interlingua-to-target-language rules, and the target language generation grammar. We start in the same way, using the source language grammar to build a randomly generated source language corpus; as shown in (Hockey et al., 2008), it is important to have a probabilistic grammar. We then use the composition of the other components to attempt to translate each source language sentence into a target language equivalent, discarding the examples for which no translation is produced. The result is an aligned bilingual corpus of arbitrary size, which can be used to train an SMT model.

We used this method to generate aligned corpora for the two MedSLT language pairs English → French and English → Japanese. For each language pair, we first generated one million source-language utterances; we next filtered them to keep only examples which were full sentences, as opposed to elliptical phrases, and finally used the translation rules and target-language generators to attempt to translate each sentence. This created approximately 305K aligned sentence-pairs for English → French (1901K words English, 1993K words French), and 311K aligned sentence-pairs for English → Japanese (1941K words English, 2214K words Japanese). We held out 2.5% of each set as development data, and 2.5% as test data. Using Giza++, Moses and SRILM (Och and Ney, 2000; Koehn et al., 2007; Stolcke, 2002), we trained SMT models from increasingly large subsets of the training portion, using the development portion in the usual way to optimize parameter values. Finally, we used the resulting models to translate the test portion.

Our primary goal was to measure the extent to which the derived versions of the SMT were able to approximate the original RBMT on data which was within the RBMT's coverage. There is a simple and natural way to perform this measurement: we apply the BLEU metric (Papineni et al., 2001), with the RBMT's translation taken as the reference. This means that perfect correspondence between the two translations would yield a BLEU score of 1.0.

This raises an important point. The BLEU scores we are using here are non-standard; they measure the extent to which the SMT approximates the RBMT, rather than, as usual, measuring

English	Is the pain above your eye?
French	Avez-vous mal au dessus des yeux?
Japanese	Itami wa me no ue no atari desu ka?
English	Have you had the pain for more than a month?
French	Avez-vous mal depuis plus d'un mois?
Japanese	Ikkagetsu ijou itami wa tsuzuki mashita ka?
English	Is the pain associated with nausea?
French	Avez-vous des nausées quand vous avez la douleur?
Japanese	Itamu to hakike wa okori masu ka?
English	Does bright light make the pain worse?
French	La douleur est-elle aggravée par une lumière forte?
Japanese	Akarui hikari wo miru to zutsu wa hidoku nari masu ka?

Table 2: Examples of English domain sentences, and the system's translations into French and Japanese.

the extent to which it approximates human translations. It is important to bring in human judgement, to evaluate the cases where the SMT and RBMT differ. If, in these cases, it transpired that human judges typically thought that the SMT was as good as the RBMT, then the difference would be purely academic. We need to satisfy ourselves that human judges typically ascribe differences between SMT and RBMT to shortcomings in the SMT rather than in the RBMT.

Concretely, we collected all the different ⟨Source, SMT-translation, RBMT-translation⟩ triples produced during the course of the experiments, and extracted those where the two translations were different. We randomly selected a set of examples for each language pair, and asked human judges to classify them into one of the following categories:

- **RBMT better:** The RBMT translation was better, in terms of preserving meaning and/or being grammatically correct;
- **SMT better:** The SMT translation was better, in terms of preserving meaning and/or being grammatically correct;
- **Similar:** Both translations were about equally good OR the source sentence was meaningless in the domain.

In order to show that our metrics are intuitively meaningful, it is sufficient to demonstrate that the frequency of occurrence of **RBMT better** is both large in comparison to that of **SMT better**, and accounts for a substantial proportion of the total population.

Finally, we consider the question of whether the SMT, which is capable of translating out-of-grammar sentences, can add useful robustness to the base system. We collected, from the set used in the experiments described in (Rayner et al., 2005), all the English sentences which failed to be translated into French. We used the best version of the English → French SMT to translate each of these sentences, and asked human judges to evaluate the translations as being clearly acceptable, clearly unacceptable, or borderline.

In the next section, we present the results of the various experiments we have just described.

4 Results

We begin with Figure 1, which shows non-standard BLEU scores for versions of the English → French SMT system trained on quantities of data increasing from 14 287 to 285 740 pairs. As can be seen, translation performance improves up to about 175 000 pairs. After this, it levels out at around BLEU = 0.90, well below that of the RBMT system with which it is being compared. A more direct way to report the result is simply to count the proportion of test sentences that are not in the training data, which are translated similarly by the SMT and the RBMT. This figure tops out at around 68%.

The results strongly suggest that the SMT is unable to replicate the RBMT's performance at all closely even in an easy language-pair, irrespective of the amount of training data available. Out of curiosity, and to reassure ourselves that the automatic generation procedure was doing something useful, we also tried training the English → French SMT on pairs derived from the 669 ut-

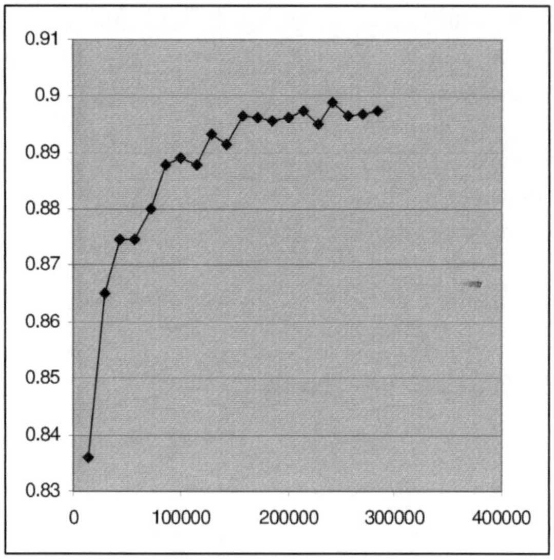

Figure 1: Non-standard BLEU scores against number of pairs of training sentences for English → French; training and test data both independently generated, hence overlapping.

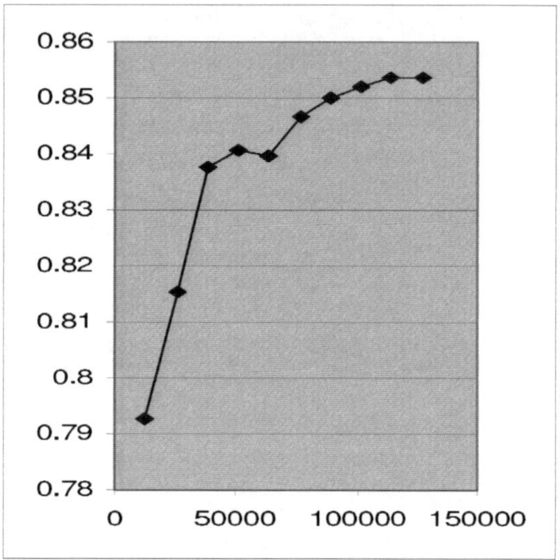

Figure 2: Non-standard BLEU scores against number of pairs of training sentences for English → French; training and test data both independently generated, then uniqued to remove duplicates and overlapping items.

terance "seed corpus" used to generate the grammar (cf. Section 2). This produced utterly dismal performance, with BLEU = 0.52. The result is more interesting than it may first appear, since, in speech recognition, the difference in performance between the SLMs trained from seed corpora and large generated corpora is fairly small (Hockey et al., 2008).

It seemed possible that the improvement in performance with increased quantities of training data might, in effect, only be due to the SMT functioning as a translation memory; since training and test data are independently generated by the same random process, they overlap, with the degree of overlap increasing as the training set gets larger. In order to investigate this hypothesis, we repeated the experiments with data which had been uniqued, so that the training and test sets were completely disjoint, and neither contained any duplicate sentences[1]. In fact, Figure 2 show that the graph for uniqued English → French data are fairly similar to the one for the original non-uniqued data shown in Figures 1. The main difference is that the non-standard BLEU score for the uniqued data, unsurprisingly, tops out at a lower level, reflecting the fact that a "translation memory" effect does indeed occur to some extent.

Results for English → Japanese showed the same trends as English → French, but were more pronounced. Table 3 compares the performance of the best versions of the SMTs for the two language-pairs, using both plain and artificially uniqued data. We see that, with plain data, the English → Japanese SMT falls even further short of replicating the performance of the RBMT than was the case for English → French; BLEU is only 0.76. The difference between the plain and uniqued versions is also more extreme. BLEU (0.64) is considerably lower for the version trained on uniqued data, suggesting that the SMT for this language pair is finding it harder to generalise, and is in effect closer to functioning as a translation memory. This is confirmed by counting the sentences in test data and not in training data which were translated similarly by the SMT and the RBMT; we find that the figure tops out at the very low value of 26%.

As noted in our discussion of the experimental framework, the non-standard BLEU scores only address the question of whether the performance of the SMT and RBMT systems is the same. It is

[1]Our opinion is that this is *not* a realistic way to evaluate the performance of a small-vocabulary system; for example, in MedSLT, one expects that at least some training sentences, e.g. "Where is the pain?", will also occur frequently in test data.

Training data	Test data	BLEU
English → French		
Generated	Generated	0.90
Gen/uniqued	Gen/uniqued	0.85
English → Japanese		
Generated	Generated	0.76
Gen/uniqued	Gen/uniqued	0.64

Table 3: Translation performance, in terms of non-standard BLEU metric, for different configurations, training on all available data of the specified type. "Generated" = data randomly generated; "Gen/uniqued" = data randomly generated, then uniqued so that duplicates are removed and test and training pairs do not overlap.

necessary to establish what the differences mean in terms of human judgements. We consequently turn to evaluation of the pairs for which the SMT and the RBMT systems produced different translation results.

Table 4 shows the categorisation, according to the criteria outlined at the end of Section 3, for 500 English → French pairs randomly selected from the set of examples where RBMT and SMT gave different results; we asked three judges to evaluate them independently, and combined their judgments by majority decision where appropriate. We observed a very heavy bias towards the RBMT, with unanimous agreement among the judges that the RBMT translation was better in 201/500 cases, and 2-1 agreement in a further 127. In contrast, there were only 4/500 cases where the judges unanimously thought that the SMT translation was preferable, with a further 12 supported by a majority decision. The rest of the table gives the cases where the RBMT and SMT translations were judged the same or cases in which the judges disagreed; there were only 41/500 cases where no majority decision was reached. Our overall conclusion is that we are justified in evaluating the SMT by using the BLEU scores with the RBMT as the reference. Of the cases where the two systems differ, only a tiny fraction, at most 16/500, indicate a better translation from the SMT, and well over half are translated better by the RBMT. Table 5 presents typical examples of bad SMT translations in the English → French pair, contrasted with the translations produced by the RBMT. The first two are grammatical errors (a superfluous extra verb in the first, and agreement errors in the second). The third is an bad choice of tense and preposition; although grammatical, the target language sentence fails to preserve the meaning, and, rather than referring to a 20 day period ending now, instead refers to a 20 day period some time in the past.

Result	Agreement	Count
RBMT better	all judges	201
RBMT better	majority	127
SMT better	all judges	4
SMT better	majority	12
Similar	all judges	34
Similar	majority	81
Unclear	disagree	41
Total		500

Table 4: Comparison of RBMT and SMT performance on 500 randomly chosen English → French translation examples, evaluated independently by three judges.

Table 6 shows a similar evaluation for the English → Japanese. Here, the difference between the SMT and RBMT versions was so pronounced that we felt justified in taking a smaller sample, of only 150 sentences. This time, 92/150 cases were unanimously judged as having a better RBMT translation, and there was not a single case where even a majority found that the SMT was better. Agreement was good here too, with only 8/150 cases not yielding at least a majority decision.

Result	Agreement	Count
RBMT better	all judges	92
RBMT better	majority	32
SMT better	all judges	0
SMT better	majority	0
Similar	all judges	2
Similar	majority	16
Unclear	disagree	8
Total		150

Table 6: Comparison of RBMT and SMT performance on 150 randomly chosen English → Japanese translation examples, evaluated independently by three judges.

Finally, we look at the performance of the SMT on material which the RBMT is not able to translate. This would seem to be a situation where

English	does a temperature change cause the headache
RBMT French	vos maux de tête sont-ils causés par des changements de température (your headaches are-they caused by changes of temperature)
SMT French	**avez-vous** vos maux de tête sont-ils causés par des changements de température (**have-you** your headaches are-they caused by changes of temperature)
English	are headaches relieved in the afternoon
RBMT French	vos maux de tête diminuent-ils l'après-midi (your headaches (MASC-PLUR) decrease-MASC-PLUR the afternoon)
SMT French	vos maux de tête **diminue-t-elle** l'après-midi (your headaches (MASC-PLUR) decrease-**FEM-SING** the afternoon)
English	have you had them for twenty days
RBMT French	avez-vous vos maux de tête depuis vingt jours (have-you your headaches since twenty days)
SMT French	avez-vous **eu** vos maux de tête **pendant** vingt jours (have-you **had** your headaches **during** twenty days)

Table 5: Examples of incorrect SMT translations from English into French. Errors are highlighted in bold.

the SMT could have an advantage; robustness is generally a strength of statistical approaches. We return to English → French in Table 7, which presents the result of running the best SMT model on the 357 examples from the test set in (Rayner et al., 2005) which failed to be translated by the RBMT. We divide the set into categories based on the reason for failure of the RBMT.

In the most populous group, translations that failed due to out of vocabulary items, the SMT was, more or less by construction, also unable to produce a translation. For the 110 items that were out of grammar coverage for the RBMT, the SMT produced 38 good translations, and another 4 borderline translations. There were 50 items that were within the source grammar coverage of the RBMT, but failed somewhere in transfer and generation processing. Of those, the majority (32) represented "bad" source sentences, considered as ill-formed for the purposes of this experiment. Out of the remaining items that were within RBMT grammar coverage, the SMT managed to produce 5 good translations and 1 borderline translation. In total, on the most lenient interpretation, the SMT produced 48 additional translations out of 357. While this improvement in recall is arguably worth having, it would come at the price of a substantial decline in precision.

Result	Count
Out of vocabulary	
Bad translation	187
Out of source grammar coverage	
Good translation	38
Bad translation	44
Borderline translation	4
Bad source sentence	34
In source grammar coverage	
Good translation	5
Bad translation	12
Borderline translation	1
Bad source sentence	32
Total	357

Table 7: English → French SMT performance on examples from the test set which failed to be translated by the RBMT, evaluated by one judge.

5 Discussion and Conclusions

We have presented a novel methodology for comparing RBMT and SMT, and tested it on a specific pair of RBMT and SMT architectures. Our claim is that these results show that the version of SMT used here is *not* in fact capable of reproducing the output of the RBMT system. Although there has been some interest in attempting to train SMT systems from RBMT output, the evaluation issues that arise when comparing SMT and RBMT versions of a high-precision limited-domain system are different from those arising in most MT tasks, and necessitate a correspondingly different methodology. It is easy to gain the impression that it is unsound, and that the experiment has been set up in such a way that only one result is possible. This is not, in fact, true.

When we have discussed the methodology with people who work primarily with SMT, we have heard two main objections. The first is that the SMT is being trained on RBMT output, and hence can only be worse; a common suggestion is that a system trained on human-produced translations could yield better results. It is not at all implausible that an SMT trained on this kind of data might perform better on material which is outside the coverage of the RBMT system. In this domain, however, the important issue is precision, not recall; what is critical is the ability to translate accurately on material that is within the constrained language defined by the RBMT coverage. The RBMT engine gives very good performance on in-coverage data, as has been shown in other evaluations of the MedSLT system, e.g. (Rayner et al., 2005); over 97% of all in-coverage sentences are correctly translated. Human-generated translations would often, no doubt, be more natural than those produced by the RBMT, and there would be slightly fewer outright mistranslations. But the primary reason why the SMT is doing badly is not that the training material contains bad translations, but rather that the SMT is incapable of correctly reproducing the translations it sees in the training data. Even in the easy English → French language-pair, the SMT often produces a different translation from the RBMT. It could *a priori* have been conceivable that the differences were uninteresting, in the sense that SMT outputs different from RBMT outputs were as good, or even better. In fact, Table 4 show that this is not true; when the two translations differ, although the SMT translation can occasionally be better, it is usually worse. Table 6 shows that this problem is considerably more acute in English → Japanese. Thus the SMT system's inability to model the RBMT system points to a real limitation.

If the SMT had instead been trained on human-generated data, its performance on in-coverage material could only have improved substantially if the SMT for some reason found it easier to learn to reproduce patterns in human-generated data than in RBMT-generated data. This seems unlikely. The SMT is being trained from a set of translation pairs which are guaranteed to be completely consistent, since they have been automatically generated by the RBMT; the fact that the RBMT system only has a small vocabulary should also work in its favour. If the SMT is unable to reproduce the RBMT's output, it is reasonable to assume it will have even greater difficulty reproducing translations present in normal human-generated training data, which is always far from consistent, and will have a larger vocabulary.

The second objection we have heard is that the non-standard BLEU scores which we have used to measure performance use the RBMT translations as a reference. People are quick to point out that, if real human translations were scored in this way, they would do less well on the non-standard metrics than the RBMT translations. This is, indeed, absolutely true, and explains why it was essential to carry out the comparison judging shown in Tables 4 and 6. If we had compared human translations with RBMT translations in the same way, we would have found that human translations which differed from RBMT translations were sometimes better, and hardly ever worse. This would have shown that the non-standard metrics were inappropriate for the task of evaluating human translations. In the actual case considered in this paper, we find a completely different pattern: the differences are one-sided in the opposite direction, indicating that the non-standard metrics do in fact agree with human judgements here.

A general objection to all these experiments is that there may be more powerful SMT architectures. We used the Giza++/Moses/SRILM combinination because it is the *de facto* standard. We have posted the data we used at `http://www.bahrc.net/geaf2009`; this will allow other groups to experiment with alternate architectures, and determine whether they do in fact yield significant improvements. For the moment, however, we think it is reasonable to claim that, in domains where high accuracy is required, it remains to be shown that SMT approaches are capable of achieving the levels of performance that rule-based systems can deliver.

References

D. Arnold, L. Balkan, S. Meijer, R.L. Humphreys, and L. Sadler. 1994. *Machine Translation: An Introductory Guide*. Blackwell, Oxford.

P. Bouillon, M. Rayner, N. Chatzichrisafis, B.A. Hockey, M. Santaholma, M. Starlander, Y. Nakao, K. Kanzaki, and H. Isahara. 2005. A generic multilingual open source platform for limited-domain medical speech translation. In *Proceedings of the 10th Conference of the European Association for Machine Translation (EAMT)*, pages 50–58, Budapest, Hungary.

P. Bouillon, F. Ehsani, R. Frederking, and M. Rayner, editors. 2006. *Proceedings of the HLT-NAACL International Workshop on Medical Speech Translation*, New York.

P. Bouillon, F. Ehsani, R. Frederking, M. McTear, and M. Rayner, editors. 2008a. *Proceedings of the COLING Workshop on Speech Processing for Safety Critical Translation and Pervasive Applications*, Manchester.

P. Bouillon, G. Flores, M. Georgescul, S. Halimi, B.A. Hockey, H. Isahara, K. Kanzaki, Y. Nakao, M. Rayner, M. Santaholma, M. Starlander, and N. Tsourakis. 2008b. Many-to-many multilingual medical speech translation on a PDA. In *Proceedings of The Eighth Conference of the Association for Machine Translation in the Americas*, Waikiki, Hawaii.

N. Chatzichrisafis, P. Bouillon, M. Rayner, M. Santaholma, M. Starlander, and B.A. Hockey. 2006. Evaluating task performance for a unidirectional controlled language medical speech translation system. In *Proceedings of the HLT-NAACL International Workshop on Medical Speech Translation*, pages 9–16, New York.

L. Dugast, J. Senellart, and P. Koehn. 2008. Can we relearn an RBMT system? In *Proceedings of the Third Workshop on Statistical Machine Translation*, pages 175–178, Columbus, Ohio.

B.A. Hockey, M. Rayner, and G. Christian. 2008. Training statistical language models from grammar-generated data: A comparative case-study. In *Proceedings of the 6th International Conference on Natural Language Processing*, Gothenburg, Sweden.

R. Jonson. 2005. Generating statistical language models from interpretation grammars in dialogue systems. In *Proceedings of the 11th EACL*, Trento, Italy.

A. Jurafsky, C. Wooters, J. Segal, A. Stolcke, E. Fosler, G. Tajchman, and N. Morgan. 1995. Using a stochastic context-free grammar as a language model for speech recognition. In *Proceedings of the IEEE International Conference on Acoustics, Speech and Signal Processing*, pages 189–192.

P. Koehn, H. Hoang, A. Birch, C. Callison-Burch, M. Federico, N. Bertoldi, B. Cowan, W. Shen, C. Moran, R. Zens, et al. 2007. Moses: Open source toolkit for statistical machine translation. In *ANNUAL MEETING-ASSOCIATION FOR COMPUTATIONAL LINGUISTICS*, volume 45, page 2.

F.J. Och and H. Ney. 2000. Improved statistical alignment models. In *Proceedings of the 38th Annual Meeting of the Association for Computational Linguistics*, Hong Kong.

K. Papineni, S. Roukos, T. Ward, and W.-J. Zhu. 2001. BLEU: a method for automatic evaluation of machine translation. Research Report, Computer Science RC22176 (W0109-022), IBM Research Division, T.J.Watson Research Center.

M. Rayner, P. Bouillon, N. Chatzichrisafis, B.A. Hockey, M. Santaholma, M. Starlander, H. Isahara, K. Kanzaki, and Y. Nakao. 2005. A methodology for comparing grammar-based and robust approaches to speech understanding. In *Proceedings of the 9th International Conference on Spoken Language Processing (ICSLP)*, pages 1103–1107, Lisboa, Portugal.

M. Rayner, B.A. Hockey, and P. Bouillon. 2006. *Putting Linguistics into Speech Recognition: The Regulus Grammar Compiler*. CSLI Press, Chicago.

M. Rayner, P. Bouillon, G. Flores, F. Ehsani, M. Starlander, B. A. Hockey, J. Brotanek, and L. Biewald. 2008. A small-vocabulary shared task for medical speech translation. In *Proceedings of the COLING Workshop on Speech Processing for Safety Critical Translation and Pervasive Applications*, Manchester.

S. Seneff, C. Wang, and J. Lee. 2006. Combining linguistic and statistical methods for bi-directional English Chinese translation in the flight domain. In *Proceedings of AMTA 2006*.

A. Stolcke. 2002. SRILM - an extensible language modeling toolkit. In *Seventh International Conference on Spoken Language Processing*. ISCA.

Y. Wilks. 2007. Stone soup and the French room. In K. Ahmad, C. Brewster, and M. Stevenson, editors, *Words and Intelligence I: Selected Papers by Yorick Wilks*, pages 255–265.

Using Large-scale Parser Output to Guide Grammar Development

Ascander Dost
Powerset, a Microsoft company
`adost@microsoft.com`

Tracy Holloway King
Powerset, a Microsoft company
`Tracy.King@microsoft.com`

Abstract

This paper reports on guiding parser development by extracting information from output of a large-scale parser applied to Wikipedia documents. Data-driven parser improvement is especially important for applications where the corpus may differ from that originally used to develop the core grammar and where efficiency concerns affect whether a new construction should be added, or existing analyses modified. The large size of the corpus in question also brings scalability concerns to the foreground.

1 Introduction

Initial development of rule-based parsers[1] is often guided by the grammar writer's knowledge of the language and test suites that cover the "core" linguistic phenomena of the language (Nerbonne et al., 1988; Cooper et al., 1996; Lehmann et al., 1996). Once the basic grammar is implemented, including an appropriate lexicon, the direction of grammar development becomes less clear. Integration of a grammar in a particular application and the use of a particular corpus can guide grammar development: the corpus and application will require the implementation of specific constructions and lexical items, as well as the reevaluation of existing analyses. To streamline this sort of output-driven development, tools to examine parser output over large corpora are necessary, and as corpus size increases, the efficiency and scalability of those tools become crucial concerns. Some immediate relevant questions for the grammar writer include:

- What constructions and lexical items need to be added for the application and corpus in question?
- For any potential new construction or lexical item, is it worth adding, or would it be better to fall back to robust techniques?
- For existing analyses, are they applying correctly, or do they need to be restricted, or even removed?

In the remainder of this section, we briefly discuss some existing techniques for guiding large-scale grammar development and then introduce the grammar being developed and the tool we use in examining the grammar's output. The remainder of the paper discusses development of lexical resources and grammar rules, how overall progress is tracked, and how analysis of the grammar output can help development in other natural language components.

1.1 Current Techniques

There are several techniques currently being used by grammar engineers to guide large-scale grammar development, including error mining to detect gaps in grammar coverage, querying tools for gold standard treebanks to determine frequency of linguistic phenomena, and tools for querying parser output to determine how linguistic phenomena were analyzed in practice.

An error mining technique presented by van Noord (2004) (henceforth: the van Noord Tool) can reveal gaps in grammar coverage by comparing the frequency of arbitrary n-grams of words in unsuccessfully parsed sentences with the same n-grams in unproblematic sentences, for large unannotated corpora.[2] A parser can be run over new text, and a comparison of the in-domain and

[1] The techniques discussed here may also be relevant to purely machine-learned parsers and are certainly applicable to hybrid parsers.

[2] The suffix array error mining software is available at: http://www.let.rug.nl/~vannoord/SuffixArrays.tgz

Proceedings of the 2009 Workshop on Grammar Engineering Across Frameworks, ACL-IJCNLP 2009, pages 63–70,
Suntec, Singapore, 6 August 2009.

out-of-domain sentences can determine, for instance, that the grammar cannot parse adjective-noun hyphenation correctly (e.g. *an electrical-switch cover*). A different technique for error mining that uses discriminative treebanking is described in (Baldwin et al., 2005). This technique aims at determining issues with lexical coverage, grammatical (rule) coverage, ungrammaticality within the corpus (e.g. misspelled words), and extragrammaticality within the corpus (e.g. bulleted lists).

A second approach involves querying gold-standard treebanks such as the Penn Treebank (Marcus et al., 1994) and Tiger Treebank (Brants et al., 2004) to determine the frequency of certain phenomena. For example, Tiger Search (Lezius, 2002) can be used to list and frequency-sort stacked prepositions (e.g. *up to the door*) or temporal noun/adverbs after prepositions (e.g. *by now*). The search tools over these treebanks allow for complex searches involving specification of lexical items, parts of speech, and tree configurations (see (Mírovský, 2008) for discussion of query requirements for searching tree and dependency banks).

The third approach we discuss here differs from querying gold-standard treebanks in that corpora of actual parser output are queried to examine how constructions are analyzed by the grammar. For example, Bouma and Kloosterman (2002) use XQuery (an XML query language) to mine parse results stored as XML data.[3] It is this sort of examination of parser output that is the focus of the present paper, and specific examples of our experiences follow in Section 2.2.

Use of such tools has proven vital to the development of large-scale grammars. Based on our experiences with them, we began extensively using a tool called Oceanography (Waterman, 2009) to search parser output for very large (approximately 125 million sentence) parse runs stored on a distributed file system. Oceanography queries the parser output and returns counts of specific constructions or properties, as well as the example sentences they were extracted from. In the subsequent sections we discuss how this tool (in conjunction with existing ones like the van Noord Tool and Tiger Search) has enhanced grammar development for an English-language Lexical-Functional Grammar used for a semantic search application over Wikipedia.

[3] See also (Bouma and Kloosterman, 2007) for further discussion of this technique.

1.2 The Grammar and its Role

The grammar being developed is a Lexical-Functional Grammar (LFG (Dalrymple, 2001)) that is part of the ParGram parallel grammar project (Butt et al., 1999; Butt et al., 2002). It runs on the XLE system (Crouch et al., 2009) and produces c(onstituent)-structures which are trees and f(unctional)-structures which are attribute value matrices recording grammatical functions and other syntactic features such as tense and number, as well as debugging features such as the source of lexical items (e.g. from a named entity finder, the morphology, or the guesser). There is a base grammar which covers the constructions found in standard written English, as well as three overlay grammars: one for parsing Wikipedia sentences, one for parsing Wikipedia headers, and one for parsing queries (sentential, phrasal, and keyword).

The grammar is being used by Powerset (a Microsoft company) in a semantic consumer-search reference vertical which allows people to search Wikipedia using natural language queries as well as traditional keyword queries. The system uses a pipeline architecture which includes: text extraction, sentence breaking, named entity detection, parsing (tokenization, morphological analysis, c-structure, f-structure, ranking), semantic analysis, and indexing of selected semantic facts (see Figure 1). A similar pipeline is used on the query side except that the resulting semantic analysis is turned into a query execution language which is used to query the index.

text extraction	*script*
sentence breaker	*finite state*
named entity detection	*MaxEnt model*
LFG grammars	
tokenizer	*finite state*
morphology	*finite state*
grammar	*XLE: parser*
ranking	*MaxEnt model*
semantics	*XLE: XFR*

Figure 1: NL Pipeline Components

The core idea behind using a deep parser in the pipeline in conjunction with the semantic rules is to localize role information as to who did what to whom (i.e. undo long-distance dependencies and locate heads of arguments), to abstract away from choice of particular lexical items (i.e. lemmatization and detection of synonyms), and generally provide a more normalized representation of the natural language string to improve both precision and recall.

1.3 Oceanography

As a byproduct of the indexing pipeline, all of the syntactic and semantic structures are stored for later inspection as part of failure analysis.[4] The files containing these structures are distributed over several machines since ∼125 million sentences are parsed for the analysis of Wikipedia.

For any given syntactic or semantic structure, the XLE ordered rewrite system (XFR; (Crouch et al., 2009)) can be used to extract information that is of interest to the grammar engineer, by way of "rules" or statements in the XFR language. As the XFR ordered rewrite system is also used for the semantics rules that turn f-structures into semantic representations, the notation is familiar to the grammar writers and is already designed for manipulating the syntactic f-structures.

However, the mechanics of accessing each file on each machine and then assembling the results is prohibitively complicated without a tool that provides a simple interface to the system. Oceanography was designed to take a single specification file stating:

- which data to examine (which corpus version; full Wikipedia build or fixed 10,000 document set);
- the XFR rules to be applied;
- what extracted data to count and report back.

Many concrete examples of Oceanography runs will be discussed below. The basic idea is to use the XFR rules to specify searches over lexical items, features, and constructions in a way that is similar to that of Tiger Search and other facilities. The Oceanography machinery enables these searches over massive data and helps in compiling the results for the grammar engineer to inspect. We believe that similar approaches would be feasible to implement in other grammar development environments and, in fact, for some grammar outputs and applications, existing tools such as Tiger Search would be sufficient. By providing examples where such searches have aided our grammar development, we hope to encourage other grammar engineers to similarly extend their efforts to use easy access to massive data to drive their work.

[4] The index is self-contained and does not need to reference the semantic, much less the earlier syntactic, structures as part of the search application.

2 Grammar Development

The ParGram English LFG grammar has been developed over many years. However, the focus of development was on newspaper text and technical manuals, although some adaptation was done for new domains (King and Maxwell, 2007). When moving to the Wikipedia domain, many new constructions and lexical items were encountered (see (Baldwin et al., 2005) for a similar experience with the BNC) and, at the same time, the requirements on parsing efficiency increased.

2.1 Lexical Development

When first parsing a new corpus, the grammar encounters new words that were previously unknown to the morphology. The morphology falls back to a guesser that uses regular expressions to guess the part of speech and other features associated with an unknown form. For example, a novel word ending in *s* might be a plural noun. The grammar records a feature _LEX-SOURCE with the value *guesser* for all guessed words. Oceanography was used to extract all guessed forms and their parts of speech. In many cases, the guesser had correctly identified the word's part of speech. However, words that occurred frequently were added to the morphology to avoid the possibility that they would be incorrectly guessed as a different part of speech. The fact that Oceanography was able to identify not just the word, but its posited part of speech and frequency in the corpus greatly sped lexical development.

Incorrect guessing of verbs was of particular concern to the grammar writers, as misidentification of verbs was almost always accompanied by a bad parse. In addition, subcategorization frames for guessed verbs were guessed as either transitive or intransitive, which often proved to be incorrect. As such, the guessed verbs extracted using Oceanography were hand curated: true verbs were added to the morphology and their subcategorization frames to the lexicon. Due to the high rate of error with guessed verbs, once the correctly guessed verbs were added to the morphology, this option was removed from the guesser.[5]

Overall, ~4200 new stems were added to the already substantial morphology, with correct inflection. Approximately ~1300 of these were verbs. The decision to eliminate verbs as possible guessed parts of speech was directly motivated by data extracted using Oceanography.

Since the guesser works with regular expressions (e.g. lowercase letters + *s* form plural nouns), it is possible to encounter forms in the corpus that neither the morphology nor the guesser recognize. The grammar will fragment on these sentences, creating well-formed f-structure chunks but no single spanning parse, and the unrecognized forms will be recorded as TOKENs (Riezler et al., 2002). An Oceanography run extracting all TOKENs resulted in the addition of several new patterns to the guesser as well as the addition of some of the frequent forms to the morphology. For example, sequences of all upper case letters followed by a hyphen and then by a sequence of digits were added for forms like *AK-47*, *F-22*, and *V-1*.

The guesser and TOKENs Oceanography runs look for general problems with the morphology and lexicon, and can be run for every new corpus. More specific jobs are run when evaluating whether to implement a new analysis, or when evaluating whether a current analysis is functioning properly. For example, use of the van Noord tool indicated that the grammar had problems with certain less common multiword prepositions (e.g. *pursuant to*, *in contrast with*). Once these multiword prepositions were added, the question then arose as to whether more common prepositions should be multiwords when stacked (e.g. *up to*, *along with*). An Oceanography run was performed to extract all occurrences of stacked prepositions from the corpus. Their frequency was tallied in both the stacked formations and when used as simple prepositions. With this information, we determined which stacked configurations to add to the lexicon as multiword prepositions, while maintaining preposition stacking for less common combinations.

2.2 Grammar Rule Development

In addition to using Oceanography to help develop the morphology and lexicon, it has also proven extremely useful in grammar rule development. In general, the issue is not in finding constructions which the grammar does not cover correctly: a quick investigation of sentences which fragment can provide these and issues are identified and reported by the semantics which uses the syntax output as its input. Furthermore, the van Noord tool can be used to effectively identify gaps in grammar rule coverage.

Rather, the more pressing issues include whether it is worthwhile adding a construction, which possible solution to pick (when it is worthwhile), and whether an existing solution is applying correctly and efficiently. Being able to look at the occurrence of a construction over large amounts of data can help with all of these issues, especially when combined with searching over gold standard treebanks such as the Penn Treebank.

Determining which constructions to examine using Oceanography is often the result of failure analysis findings on components outside the grammar itself, but that build on the grammar's output later in the natural language processing pipeline. The point we wish to emphasize here is that the grammar engineer's effectiveness can greatly benefit from being able to take a set of problematic data gathered from massive parser output and determine from it that a particular construction merits closer scrutiny.

2.2.1 *When* relative/subordinate clauses

An observation that subordinate clauses containing *when* (e.g. *Mary laughed when Ed tripped.*) were sometimes misanalyzed as relative clauses attaching to a noun (e.g. *the time when Ed tripped*) prompted a more directed analysis of whether *when* relative clauses should be allowed to attach to nouns that were not time-related expressions (e.g. *time, year, day*). An Oceanography run was performed to extract all *when* relative clauses, the modified nominal head, and the sentence containing the construction. A frequency-sorted list of nouns taking *when* relative clause modifiers helped to direct hand-examination of *when* relative clauses for accuracy of the analysis. This yielded some correct analyses:

(1) There are **times** [when a Bigfoot sighting or footprint is a hoax].

More importantly, however, the search revealed many incorrect analyses of *when* subordinate

[5] It is simple to turn the guessed verbs back on in order to run the same Oceanography experiment with a new corpus.

clauses as relative clauses:

(2) He gets the last **laugh** [when he tows away his boss' car as well as everyone else's].

By extracting all *when* relative clauses, and their head nouns, it was determined that the construction was generally only correct for a small class of time expression nominals. Comparatively, *when* relative clause modification of other nominals was rarely correct. The grammar was modified to disprefer relative clause analyses of *when* clauses unless the head noun was an expression of time. As a result, the overall quality of parses for all sentences containing *when* subordinate clauses was improved.

2.2.2 Relative clauses modifying gerunds

Another example of an issue with the accuracy of a grammatical analysis concerns gerund nouns modified by relative clauses without an overt relative pronoun (e.g. *the singing we liked*). It was observed that many strings were incorrectly analyzed as a gerund and reduced relative clause modifier:

(3) She lost all of her powers, **including** [her sonic screams].

Again, a frequency sorted list of gerunds modified by reduced relative clauses helped to guide hand inspection of the instances of this construction. By extracting all of the gerunds with reduced relative clause modifiers, it was possible to see which gerunds were appearing in this construction (e.g. *including* occurred alarmingly frequently) and how rarely the overall analysis was correct. As a result of the data analysis, such relative clause modifiers are now dispreferred in the grammar and certain verbs (e.g. *include*) are additionally dispreferred as gerunds in general. Note that this type of failure analysis is not possible with a tool (such as the van Noord tool) that only points out gaps in grammar coverage.

2.2.3 Noun-noun compounds

As part of the semantic search application, argument-relation triples are extracted from the corpus and presented to the user as a form of summary over what Wikipedia knows about a particular entity. These are referred to as *Factz*. For example, a search on *Noam Chomsky* will find Factz triples as in Figure 2. Such an application highlights parse problems, since the predicate-argument relations displayed are ultimately extracted from the syntactic parses themselves.

One class of problem arises when forms which are ambiguous between nominal and verbal analyses are erroneously analyzed as verbs and hence show up as Factz relations. This is particularly troublesome when the putative verb is part of a noun-noun compound (e.g. *ice cream, hot dog*) and the verb form is comparatively rare. A list of potentially problematic noun-noun compounds was extracted by using an independent part of speech tagger over the sentences that generated the Factz triples. If the relation in the triple was tagged as a noun and was not a deverbal noun (e.g. *destruction, writing*), then the first argument of the triple and the relation were tagged as potentially problematic noun-noun compounds. Oceanography was then used to determine the relative frequency of whether the word pairs were analyzed as noun-noun compounds, verb-argument relations, or independent nouns and verbs.

This distributional information, in conjunction with information about known noun-noun compounds in WordNet (Fellbaum, 1998), is being used to extract a set of ~100,000 noun-noun compounds whose analysis is extremely strongly preferred by the grammar. Currently, these are constrained via c-structure optimality marks[6] but they may eventually be allowed only as noun-noun compounds if the list proves reliable enough.

3 Tracking Grammar Progress

The grammar is used as part of a larger application which is actively being developed and which is regularly updated. As such, new versions of the grammar are regularly released. Each release includes a detailed list of improvements and bug fixes, as well as requirements on other components of the system (e.g. the grammar may require a specific version of the XLE parser or of the morphology). It is extremely important to be able to confirm that the changes to the grammar are in place and are functioning as expected when used in the pipeline. Some changes can be confirmed by browsing documents, finding a sentence likely to contain the relevant lexical item or construction, and then inspecting the syntactic structures for that

[6]See (Frank et al., 2001) and (Crouch et al., 2009) on the use of Optimality Theory marks within XLE. C-structure optimality marks apply preferences to the context free backbone before any constraints supplied by the f-structure annotations are applied. This means that the noun-noun compounds will be the only analysis possible if any tree can be constructed with them.

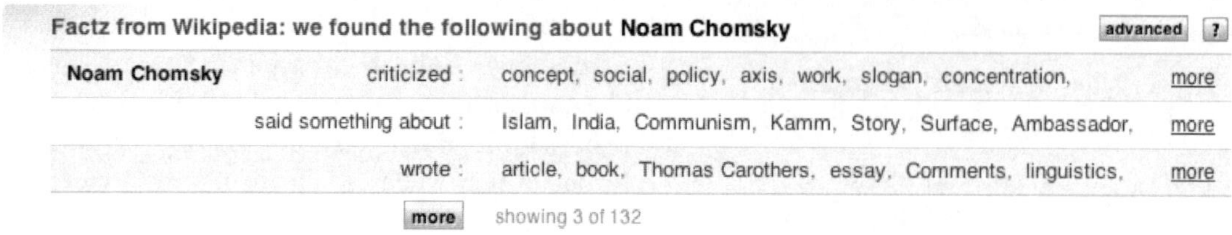

Figure 2: Example Factz

document.

3.1 Confirming Grammar Changes

However, some changes are more complicated to confirm either because it is hard to determine from a sentence whether the grammar change would apply or because the change is more frequency related. For these types of changes, Oceanography runs can detect whether a rare change occurred at all, alleviating the need to search through documents by hand. For example, to determine whether the currency symbols are being correctly treated by the grammar, especially the ones that are not standard ASCII (e.g. the euro and yen symbols), two simple XFR rules can be written: one that looks for the relevant c-structure leaf node and counts up which symbols occur under this node and one that looks for the known list of currency symbols in the f-structure and counts up what part-of-speech they were analyzed as.

To detect whether frequency related changes to the grammar are behaving as expected, two Oceanography runs can be compared, one with the older grammar and one with the newer one. For example, to determine whether relative clauses headed by *when* were dispreferred relative to subordinate clauses, the number of such relative clauses and such subordinate clauses were counted in two successive runs; the relative occurrence of the types confirmed that the preference mechanism was working correctly. In addition, a quick examination of sentences containing each type showed that the change was not over-applying (e.g. incorrectly analyzing *when* relative clauses as subordinate clauses).

3.2 General Grammar Checking

In addition to Oceanography runs done to check on specific changes to the grammar, a core set of XFR rules extracts all of the features from the f-structure and counts them. The resulting statistics of features and counts are computed for each major release and compared to that of the previous release. This provides a list of new features which subsequent components must be alerted to (e.g. a feature added to indicate what type of punctuation surrounded a parenthetical). It also provides a quick check of whether some feature is no longer occurring with the same frequency. In some cases this is expected; once many guessed forms were added to the lexicon, the feature indicating that the guesser had applied dropped sharply. However, unexpected steep variations from previous runs can be investigated to make sure that rules were not inadvertently removed from the grammar, and that rules added to the grammar are functioning correctly.

4 Using Grammar Output to Develop Other Components

In addition to being used in development of the grammar itself, examination of the grammar output can be useful for engineering efforts on other components. In addition to the examples cited above concerning the development of the morphology used by the grammar, we discuss one simple example here. The sentence breaker used in the pipeline is designed for high precision; it only breaks sentences when it is sure that there is a sentence break. To make up for breaks that may have been missed, the grammar contains a rule that allows multiple sentences to be parsed as a single string. The resulting f-structure has the final sentence's f-structure as the value of a feature, LAST, and the remainder as the value of a feature, REST. The grammar iteratively parses multiple sentences into these LAST-REST structures. Because the feature LAST is only instantiated when parsing multiple sentences, input strings whose parses contained a LAST component could be extracted to determine whether the sentence breaker's behavior should be changed. An example of two sentences which were not broken is:

(4) The current air staff includes former CNN Headline News gal Holly Firfer in the mornings with co-host Orff. Mid-days is Mara Davis, who does a theme lunch hour.

The relatively short unknown word *Orff* before the period makes it unclear whether this is an abbreviation or not. Based on the Oceanography analysis, the number of unbroken sentences which received analyses was roughly halved and one bug concerning footnote markers was discovered and fixed.

5 Conclusion

Large-scale grammars are increasingly being used in applications. In order to maximize their effectiveness in terms of coverage, accuracy, and efficiency for a given application, it is increasingly important to examine the behavior of the grammar on the relevant corpus and in the relevant application.

Having good tools makes the grammar engineer's task of massive data driven grammar development significantly easier. In this paper we have discussed how such a tool, which can apply search patterns over the syntactic (and semantic) representations of Wikipedia, is being used in a semantic search research vertical. When used in conjunction with existing tools for detecting gaps in parser coverage (e.g. the van Noord tool), Oceanography greatly aids in the evaluation of existing linguistic analyses from the parser. In addition, oceanography provides vital information to determining whether or not to implement coverage for a particular construction, based on efficiency requirements. Thus, the grammar writer has a suite of tools available to address the questions raised in the introduction of this paper: what gaps exist in parser coverage, how to best address those gaps, and whether existing analyses are functioning appropriately. We hope that our experiences encourage other grammar engineers to use similar techniques in their grammar development efforts.

Acknowledgments

We would like to thank Scott Waterman for creating Oceanography and adapting it to our needs.

References

Timothy Baldwin, John Beavers, Emily M. Bender, Dan Flickinger, Ara Kim, and Stephan Oepen. 2005. Beauty and the beast: What running a broad-coverage precision grammar over thee bnc taught us about the grammar — and the corpus. In Stephan Kepser and Marga Reis, editors, *Linguistic Evidence: Empirical, Theoretical, and Computational Perspectives*, pages 49–70. Mouton de Gruyter, Berlin.

Gosse Bouma and Geert Kloosterman. 2002. Querying dependency treebanks in XML. In *Proceedings of the Third international conference on Language Resources and Evaluation (LREC)*, Gran Canaria.

Gosse Bouma and Geert Kloosterman. 2007. Mining syntactically annotated corpora using XQuery. In *Proceedings of the Linguistic Annotation Workshop*, Prague, June. ACL.

Sabine Brants, Stefanie Dipper, Peter Eisenberg, Silvia Hansen, Esther König, Wolfgang Lezius, Christian Rohrer, George Smith, and Hans Uszkoreit. 2004. TIGER: Linguistic interpretation of a German corpus. *Research on Language and Computation*, 2:597–620.

Miriam Butt, Tracy Holloway King, María-Eugenia Niño, and Frédérique Segond. 1999. *A Grammar Writer's Cookbook*. CSLI Publications.

Miram Butt, Helge Dyvik, Tracy Holloway King, Hiroshi Masuichi, and Christian Rohrer. 2002. The Parallel Grammar Project. In *COLING2002 Workshop on Grammar Engineering and Evaluation*, pages 1–7.

Robin Cooper, Dick Crouch, Jan van Eijck, Chris Fox, Josef van Genabith, Jan Jaspars, Hans Kamp, David Milward, Manfred Pinkal, Massimo Poesio, and Steve Pulman. 1996. Using the framework. FraCas: A Framework for Computational Semantics (LRE 62-051).

Dick Crouch, Mary Dalrymple, Ronald Kaplan, Tracy Holloway King, John T. Maxwell III, and Paula Newman. 2009. XLE Documentation. Online.

Mary Dalrymple. 2001. *Lexical Functional Grammar*. Syntax and Semantics. Academic Press.

Christiane Fellbaum, editor. 1998. *WordNet: An Electronic Lexical Database*. The MIT Press.

Anette Frank, Tracy Holloway King, Jonas Kuhn, and John T. Maxwell III. 2001. Optimality theory style constraint ranking in large-scale LFG grammars. In Peter Sells, editor, *Formal and Empirical Issues in Optimality Theoretic Syntax*, pages 367–397. CSLI Publications.

Tracy Holloway King and John T. Maxwell, III. 2007. Overlay mechanisms for multi-level deep processing applications. In *Proceedings of the Grammar Engineering Across Frameworks (GEAF07) Workshop*. CSLI Publications.

Sabine Lehmann, Stephan Oepen, Sylvie Regnier-Prost, Klaus Netter, Veronika Lux, Judith Klein, Kirsten Falkedal, Frederik Fouvry, Dominique Estival, Eva Dauphin, Hervé Compagnion, Judith Baur, Lorna Balkan, and Doug Arnold. 1996. TSNLP — Test Suites for Natural Language Processing. In *Proceedings of COLING 1996.*

Wolfgang Lezius. 2002. *Ein Suchwerkzeug für syntaktisch annotierte Textkorpora (in German).* Ph.D. thesis, IMS, University of Stuttgart Arbeitspapiere des Instituts für Maschinelle Sprachverarbeitung (AIMS). volume 8, number 4.

Mitchell Marcus, Grace Kim, Mary Ann Marcinkiewicz, Robert MacIntyre, Ann Bies, Mark Ferguson, Karen Katz, and Britta Schasberger. 1994. The Penn treebank: Annotating predicate argument structure. In *ARPA Human Language Technology Workshop.*

Jiří Mírovský. 2008. PDT 2.0 requirements on a query language. In *Proceedings of ACL-08: HLT*, pages 37–45. Association for Computational Linguistics.

John Nerbonne, Dan Flickinger, and Tom Wasow. 1988. The HP Labs natural language evaluation tool. In *Proceedings of the Workshop on Evaluation of Natural Language Processing Systems.*

Stefan Riezler, Tracy Holloway King, Ronald Kaplan, Dick Crouch, John T. Maxwell III, and Mark Johnson. 2002. Parsing the Wall Street Journal using a lexical-functional grammar and discriminative estimation techniques. In *Proceedings of the ACL.*

Gertjan van Noord. 2004. Error mining for wide-coverage grammar engineering. In *Proceedings of ACL.*

Scott A. Waterman. 2009. Distributed parse mining. In *Proceedings of the NAACL Workshop on Software Engineering, Testing, and Quality Assurance for Natural Language Processing.*

A generalized method for iterative error mining in parsing results

Daniël de Kok
University of Groningen
d.j.a.de.kok@rug.nl

Jianqiang Ma
University of Groningen
j.ma@student.rug.nl

Gertjan van Noord
University of Groningen
g.j.m.van.noord@rug.nl

Abstract

Error mining is a useful technique for identifying forms that cause incomplete parses of sentences. We extend the iterative method of Sagot and de la Clergerie (2006) to treat n-grams of an arbitrary length. An inherent problem of incorporating longer n-grams is data sparseness. Our new method takes sparseness into account, producing n-grams that are as long as necessary to identify problematic forms, but not longer.

Not every cause for parsing errors can be captured effectively by looking at word n-grams. We report on an algorithm for building more general patterns for mining, consisting of words and part of speech tags.

It is not easy to evaluate the various error mining techniques. We propose a new evaluation metric which will enable us to compare different error miners.

1 Introduction

In the past decade wide-coverage grammars and parsers have been developed for various languages, such as the Alpino parser and grammar (Bouma et al., 2001) for Dutch and the English Resource Grammar (Copestake and Flickinger, 2000). Such grammars account for a large number of grammatical and lexical phenomena, and achieve high accuracies. Still, they are usually tailored to general domain texts and fail to reach the same accuracy for domain-specific texts, due to missing lexicon entries, fixed expressions, and grammatical constructs. When parsing new texts there are usually two types of parsing errors:

- The parser returns an incorrect parse. While the parser may have constructed the correct parse, the disambiguation model chose an incorrect parse.
- The parser can not find an analysis that spans the full sentence. If that sentence is allowed in the language, the grammar or lexicon is incomplete.

While the first type of errors can be alleviated by improving the disambiguation model, the second type of problems requires extension of the grammar or lexicon. Finding incomplete descriptions by hand can become a tedious task once a grammar has wide coverage. Error mining techniques aim to find problematic words or n-grams automatically, allowing the grammar developer to focus on frequent and highly suspicious forms first.

2 Previous work

In the past, two major error mining techniques have been developed by Van Noord (2004) and Sagot and de la Clergerie (2006). In this paper we propose a generalized error miner that combines the strengths of these methods. Both methods follow the same basic principle: first, a large (unannotated) corpus is parsed. After parsing, the sentences can be split up in a list of parsable and a list of unparsable sentences. Words or n-grams that occur in the list of unparsable sentences, but that do not occur in the list of parsable sentences have a high suspicion of being the cause of the parsing error.

2.1 Suspicion as a ratio

Van Noord (2004) defines the suspicion of a word as a ratio:

$$S(w) = \frac{C(w|error)}{C(w)} \tag{1}$$

where $C(w)$ is the number of occurrences of word w in all sentences, and $C(w|error)$ is the

Proceedings of the 2009 Workshop on Grammar Engineering Across Frameworks, ACL-IJCNLP 2009, pages 71–79,
Suntec, Singapore, 6 August 2009. ©2009 ACL and AFNLP

number of occurrences of w in unparsable sentences. Of course, it is often useful to look at n-grams as well. For instance, Van Noord (2004) gives an example where the word *via* had a low suspicion after parsing a corpus with the Dutch Alpino parser, while the Dutch expression *via via* (via a complex route) was unparsable.

To account for such phenomena, the notion of suspicion is extended to n-grams:

$$S(w_i..w_j) = \frac{C(w_i..w_j|error)}{C(w_i..w_j)} \quad (2)$$

Where a longer sequence $w_h...w_i...w_j...w_k$ is only considered if its suspicion is higher than each of its substrings:

$$S(w_h...w_i...w_j...w_k) > S(w_i...w_j) \quad (3)$$

While this method works well for forms that are unambiguously suspicious, it also gives forms that just happened to occur often in unparsable sentences by 'bad luck' a high suspicion. If the occurrences in unparsable sentences were accompanied by unambiguously suspicious forms, there is even more reason to believe that the form is not problematic. However, in such cases this error mining method will still assign a high suspicion to such forms.

2.2 Iterative error mining

The error mining method described by Sagot and de la Clergerie (2006) alleviates the problem of 'accidentally suspicious' forms. It does so by taking the following characteristics of suspicious forms into account:

- If a form occurs within parsable sentences, it becomes less likely that the form is the cause of a parsing error.
- The suspicion of a form should depend on the suspicions of other forms in the unparsable sentences in which it occurs.
- A form observed in a shorter sentence is initially more suspicious than a form observed in a longer sentence.

To be able to handle the suspicion of a form within its context, this method introduces the notion of *observation suspicion*, which is the suspicion of a form within a given sentence. The suspicion of a form, outside the context of a sentence, is then defined to be the average of all observation suspicions:

$$S_f = \frac{1}{|O_f|} \sum_{o_{i,j} \in O_f} S_{i,j} \quad (4)$$

Here O_f is the set of all observations of the form f, $o_{i,j}$ is the jth form of the ith sentence, and $S_{i,j}$ is the observation suspicion of $o_{i,j}$. The observation suspicions themselves are dependent on the form suspicions, making the method an iterative process. The suspicion of an observation is the suspicion of its form, normalized by suspicions of other forms occurring within the same sentence:

$$S_{i,j}^{(n+1)} = error(s_i) \frac{S_{F(o_{i,j})}^{(n+1)}}{\sum_{1 \leq j \leq |S_i|} S_{F(o_{i,j})}^{(n+1)}} \quad (5)$$

Here $error(s_i)$ is the sentence error rate, which is normally set to 0 for parsable sentences and 1 for unparsable sentences. $S_{F(o_{i,j})}$ is the suspicion of the form of observation $o_{i,j}$.

To accommodate the iterative process, we will have to redefine the form suspicion to be dependent on the observation suspicions of the previous cycle:

$$S_f^{(n+1)} = \frac{1}{|O_f|} \sum_{o_{i,j} \in O_f} S_{i,j}^{(n)} \quad (6)$$

Since there is a recursive dependence between the suspicions and the observation suspicions, starting and stopping conditions need to be defined for this cyclic process. The observation suspicions are initialized by uniformly distributing suspicion over observed forms within a sentence:

$$S_{i,j}^{(0)} = \frac{error(s_i)}{|S_i|} \quad (7)$$

The mining is stopped when the process reaches a fixed point where suspicions have stabilized.

This method solves the 'suspicion by accident' problem of ratio-based error mining. However, the authors of the paper have only used this method to mine on unigrams and bigrams. They note that they have tried mining with longer n-grams, but encountered data sparseness problems. Their paper does not describe criteria to determine when to use unigrams and when to use bigrams to represent forms within a sentence.

3 N-gram expansion

3.1 Inclusion of n-grams

While the iterative miner described by Sagot and de la Clergerie (2006) only mines on unigrams and bigrams, our prior experience with the miner described by Van Noord (2004) has shown that including longer n-grams in the mining process can capture many additional phenomena. To give one example: the words *de* (*the*), *eerste* (*first*), and *beste* (*best*) had very low suspicions during error mining, while the trigram *eerste de beste* had a very high suspicion. This trigram occurred in the expression *de eerste de beste* (*the first you can find*). While the individual words within this expression were described by the lexicon, this multiword expression was not.

3.2 Suspicion sharing

It may seem to be attractive to include all n-grams within a sentence in the mining process. However, this is problematic due to *suspicion sharing*. For instance, consider the trigram w_1, w_2, w_3 in which w_2 is the cause of a parsing error. In this case, the bigrams w_1, w_2 and w_2, w_3 will become suspicious, as well as the trigram w_1, w_2, w_3. Since there will be multiple very suspicious forms within the same sentence the unigram w_2 will have no opportunity to manifest itself.

A more practical consideration is that the number of forms within a sentence grows at such a rate $(n + (n-1) ... + 1)$ that error mining becomes unfeasible for large corpora, both in time and in space.

3.3 Expansion method

To avoid suspicion sharing we have devised a method for adding and expanding n-grams when it is deemed useful. This method iterates through a sentence of unigrams, and expands unigrams to longer n-grams when there is evidence that it is useful. This expansion step is a preprocessor to the iterative miner, that uses the same iterative algorithm as described by Sagot and De la Clergerie. Within this preprocessor, suspicion is defined in the same manner as in Van Noord (2004), as a ratio of occurrences in unparsable sentences and the total number of occurrences.

The motivation behind this method is that there can be two expansion scenarios. When we have the bigram w_1, w_2, either one of the unigrams can be problematic or the bigram w_1, w_2. In the former case, the bigram w_1, w_2 will also inherit the high suspicion of the problematic unigram. In the latter case, the bigram will have a higher suspicion than both of its unigrams. Consequently, we want to expand the unigram w_1 to the bigram w_1, w_2 if the bigram is more suspicious than both of its unigrams. If w_1, w_2 is equally suspicious as one of its unigrams, it is not useful to expand to a bigram since we want to isolate the cause of the parsing error as much as possible.

The same methodology is followed when we expand to longer n-grams. Expansion of w_1, w_2 to the trigram w_1, w_2, w_3 will only be permitted if w_1, w_2, w_3 is more suspicious than its bigrams. Since the suspicion of w_3 aggregates to w_2, w_3, we account for both w_3 and w_2, w_3 in this comparison.

The general algorithm is that the expansion to an n-gram $i..j$ is allowed when $S(i..j) > S(i..j-1)$ and $S(i..j) > S(i+1..j)$. This gives us a sentence that is represented by the n-grams $n_0..n_x$, $n_1..n_y$, ... $n_{|s_i|-1}..n_{|s_i|-1}$.

3.4 Data sparseness

While initial experiments with the expansion algorithm provided promising results, the expansion algorithm was too eager. This eagerness is caused by data sparseness. Since longer n-grams occur less frequently, the suspicion of an n-gram occurring in unparsable sentences goes up with the length of the n-gram until it reaches its maximum value. The expansion conditions do not take this effect into account.

To counter this problem, we have introduced an expansion factor. This factor depends on the frequency of an n-gram within unparsable sentences and asymptotically approaches one for higher frequencies. As a result more burden of proof is inflicted upon the expansion: the longer n-gram either needs to be relatively frequent, or it needs to be much more suspicious than its (n-1)-grams. The expansion conditions are changed to $S(i..j) > S(i..j-1) \cdot extFactor$ and $S(i..j) > S(i+1..j) \cdot extFactor$, where

$$extFactor = 1 + e^{-\alpha |O_{f,unparsable}|} \quad (8)$$

In our experiments $\alpha = 1.0$ proved to be a good setting.

3.5 Pattern expansion

Previous work on error mining was primarily focused on the extraction of interesting word n-grams. However, it could also prove useful to allow for patterns consisting of other information than words, such as part of speech tags or lemmas. We have done preliminary work on the integration of part of speech tags during the n-gram expansion. We use the same methodology as word-based n-gram expansion, however we also consider expansion with a part of speech tag.

Since we are interested in building patterns that are as general as possible, we expand the pattern with a part of speech tag if that creates a more suspicious pattern. Expansion with a word is attempted if expansion with a part of speech tag is unsuccessful. E.g., if we attempt to expand the word bigram w_1w_2, we first try the tag expansion $w_1w_2t_3$. This expansion is allowed when $S(w_1, w_2, t_3) > S(w_1, w_2) \cdot extFactor$ and $S(w_1, w_2, t_3) > S(w_2, t_3) \cdot extFactor$. If the expansion is not allowed, then expansion to $S(w1, w2, w3)$ is attempted. As a result, mixed patterns emerge that are as general as possible.

4 Implementation

4.1 Compact representation of data

To be able to mine large corpora some precautions need to be made. During the n-gram expansion stage, we need quick access to the frequencies of arbitrary length n-grams. Additionally, all unparsable sentences have to be kept in memory, since we have to traverse them for n-gram expansion. Ordinary methods for storing n-gram frequencies (such as hash tables) and data will not suffice for large corpora.

As Van Noord (2004) we used perfect hashing to restrict memory use, since hash codes are generally shorter than the average token length. Additionally, comparisons of numbers are much faster than comparisons of strings, which speeds up the n-gram expansion step considerably.

During the n-gram expansion step the miner calculates ratio-based suspicions of n-grams using frequencies of an n-gram in parsable and unparsable sentences. The n-gram can potentially have the length of a whole sentence, so it is not practical to store n-gram ratios in a hash table. Instead, we compute a suffix array (Manber and Myers, 1990) for the parsable and unparsable sentences[1]. A suffix array is an array that contains indices pointing to sequences in the data array, that are ordered by suffix.

We use suffix arrays differently than Van Noord (2004), because our expansion algorithm requires the parsable and unparsable frequencies of the (n-1)-grams, and the second (n-1)-gram is not (necessarily) adjacent to the n-gram in the suffix array. As such, we require random access to frequencies of n-grams occurring in the corpus. We can compute the frequency of any n-gram by looking up its upper and lower bounds in the suffix array[2], where the difference is the frequency.

4.2 Determining ratios for pattern expansion

While suffix arrays provide a compact and relatively fast data structure for looking up n-gram frequencies, they are not usable for pattern expansion (see section 3.5). Since we need to look up frequencies of every possible combination of representations that are used, we would have to create d^l suffix arrays to be (theoretically) able to look up pattern frequencies with the same time complexity, where d is the number of dimensions and l is the corpus length.

For this reason, we use a different method for calculating pattern frequencies. First, we build a hash table for each type of information that can be used in patterns. A hash table contains an instance of such information as a key (e.g. a specific word or part of speech tag) and a set of corpus indices where the instance occurred in the corpus as the value associated with that key. Now we can look up the frequency of a sequence $i..j$ by calculating the set intersection of the indices of j and the indices found for the sequence $i..j-1$, after incrementing the indices of $i..j-1$ by one.

The complexity of calculating frequencies following this method is linear, since the set of indices for a given instance can be retrieved with a $O(1)$ time complexity, while both incrementing the set indices and set intersection can be performed in $O(n)$ time. However, n can be very large: for instance, the start of sentence marker forms a substantial part of the corpus and is looked up once for every sentence. In our implementation we limit the time spent on such patterns by caching very frequent bigrams in a hash table.

4.3 Removing low-suspicion forms

Since normally only one form within a sentence will be responsible for a parsing error, many forms will have almost no suspicion at all. However, during the mining process, their suspicions will be recalculated during every cycle. Mining can be sped up considerably by removing forms that have a negligible suspicion.

[1]We use the suffix sorting algorithm by Peter M. McIlroy and M. Douglas McIlroy.

[2]Since the suffix array is sorted, finding the upper and lower bounds is a binary search in $O(log\ n)$ time.

If we do not drop forms, mining of the Dutch Wikipedia corpus described in section 5.3, with n-gram expansion and the extension factor enabled, resulted in 4.8 million forms with 13.4 million form observations in unparsable sentences. If we mine the same material and drop forms with a suspicion below 0.001 there were 3.5 million forms and 4.0 million form observations within unparsable sentences left at the end of the iterative mining process.

5 Evaluation

5.1 Methodology

In previous articles, error mining methods have primarily been evaluated manually. Both Van Noord (2004) and Sagot and de la Clergerie (2006) make a qualitative analysis of highly suspicious forms. But once one starts experimenting with various extensions, such as n-gram expansion and expansion factor functions, it is difficult to qualify changes through small-scale qualitative analysis.

To be able to evaluate changes to the error miner, we have supplemented qualitative analysis with a automatic quantitative evaluation method. Since error miners are used by grammar engineers to correct a grammar or lexicon by hand, the evaluation metric should model this use case:

- We are interested in seeing problematic forms that account for errors in a large number of unparsable sentences first.
- We are only interested in forms that actually caused the parsing errors. Analysis of forms that do not, or do not accurately pinpoint origin of the parsing errors costs a lot of time.

These requirements map respectively to the recall and precision metrics from information retrieval:

$$P = \frac{|\{S_{unparsable}\} \cap \{S_{retrieved}\}|}{|\{S_{retrieved}\}|} \quad (9)$$

$$R = \frac{|\{S_{unparsable}\} \cap \{S_{retrieved}\}|}{|\{S_{unparsable}\}|} \quad (10)$$

Consequently, we can also calculate the f-score (van Rijsbergen, 1979):

$$F - score = \frac{(1 + \beta^2) \cdot (P \cdot R)}{(\beta^2 \cdot P + R)} \quad (11)$$

The f-score is often used with $\beta = 1.0$ to give as much weight to precision as recall. In evaluating error mining, this can permit cheating. For instance, consider an error mining that recalls the start of sentence marker as the first problematic form. Such a strategy would instantly give a recall of 1.0, and if the coverage of a parser for a corpus is relatively low, a relatively good initial f-score will be obtained. Since error mining is often used in situations where coverage is still low, we give more bias to precision by using $\beta = 0.5$.

We hope to provide more evidence in the future that this evaluation method indeed correlates with human evaluation. But in our experience it has the required characteristics for the evaluation of error mining. For instance, it is resistant to recalling of different or overlapping n-grams from the same sentences, or recalling n-grams that occur often in both parsable and unparsable sentences.

5.2 Scoring methods

After error mining, we can extract a list of forms and suspicions, and order the forms by their suspicion. But normally we are not only interested in forms that are the most suspicious, but forms that are suspicious and frequent. Sagot and de la Clergerie (2006) have proposed three scoring methods that can be used to rank forms:

- Concentrating on suspicions: $M_f = S_f$
- Concentrating on most frequent potential errors: $M_f = S_f|O_f|$
- Balancing between these possibilities: $M_f = S_f \cdot ln|O_f|$

For our experiments, we have replaced the observation frequencies of the form ($|O_f|$) by the frequency of observations within unparsable sentences ($|\{O_{f,unparsable}\}|$). This avoids assigning a high score to very frequent unsuspicious forms.

5.3 Material

In our experiments we have used two corpora that were parsed with the wide-coverage Alpino parser and grammar for Dutch:

- Quantitative evaluation was performed on the Dutch Wikipedia of August 2008[3]. This corpus consists of 7 million sentences (109 million words). For 8.4% of the sentences no full analysis could be found.

[3]http://ilps.science.uva.nl/WikiXML/

- A qualitative evaluation of the extensions was performed on the Flemish Mediargus newspaper corpus (up to May 31, 2007)[4]. This corpus consists of 67 million sentences (1.1 billion words). For 9.2% of the sentences no full analysis could be found.

Flemish is a variation of Dutch written and spoken in Belgium, with a grammar and lexicon that deviates slightly from standard Dutch. Previously, the Alpino grammar and lexicon was never specifically modified for parsing Flemish.

6 Results

6.1 Iterative error mining

We have evaluated the different mining methods with the three scoring functions discussed in section 5.2. In the results presented in this section we only list the results with the scoring function that performed best for a given error mining method (section 6.3 provides an overview of the best scoring functions for different mining methods).

Our first interest was if, and how much iterative error mining outperforms error mining with suspicion as a ratio. To test this, we compared the method described by Van Noord (2004) and the iterative error miner of Sagot and de la Clergerie (2006). For the iterative error miner we evaluated both on unigrams, and on unigrams and bigrams where all unigrams and bigrams are used (without further selection). Figure 6.1 shows the f-scores for these miners after *N* retrieved forms.

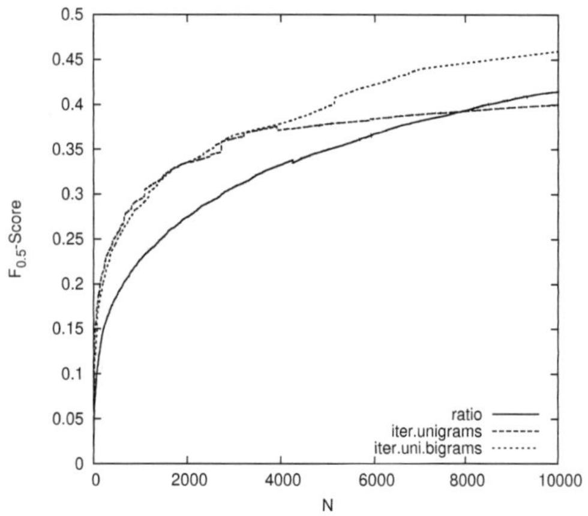

Figure 1: F-scores after retrieving N forms for ratio-based mining, iterative mining on unigrams and iterative mining on uni- and bigrams.

[4]http://www.mediargus.be/

The unigram iterative miner outperforms the ratio-based miner during the retrieval of the first 8000 forms. The f-score graph of the iterative miner on unigrams flattens after retrieving about 4000 forms. At that point unigrams are not specific enough anymore to pinpoint more sophisticated problems. The iterative miner on uni- and bigrams performs better than the ratio-based miner, even beyond 8000 forms. More importantly, the curves of the iterative miners are steeper. This is relevant if we consider that a grammar engineer will only look at a few thousands of forms. For instance, the ratio-based miner achieves an f-score of 0.4 after retrieving 8448 forms, while the iterative miner on uni- and bigrams attains the same f-score after retrieving 5134 forms.

6.2 N-gram expansion

In our second experiment we have compared the performance of iterative mining on uni- and bigrams with an iterative miner using the n-gram expansion algorithm described in section 3. Figure 6.2 shows the result of n-gram expansion compared to mining just uni- and bigrams. Both the results for expansion with and without use of the expansion factor are shown.

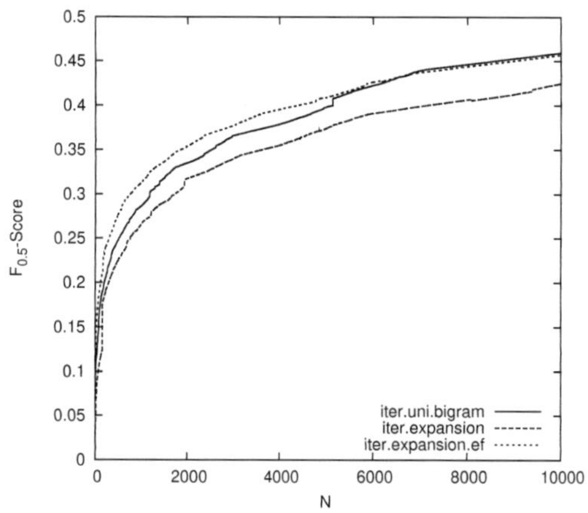

Figure 2: F-scores after retrieving N forms for iterative mining on uni- and bigrams, and iterative mining using n-gram expansion with and without using an expansion factor.

We can see that the expansion to longer n-grams gives worse results than mining on uni- and bigrams when data sparseness is not accounted for. The expansion stage will select forms that may be accurate, but that are more specific than needed. As such, the recall per retrieved form is lower on average, as can be seen in figure 6.2. But if sparseness is taken into account through the use of the expansion factor, we achieve higher f-scores than mining on uni- and bigrams up to the retrieval of circa five thousand forms. Since a user of an error mining tool will probably only look at the first few thousands of forms, this is a welcome improvement.

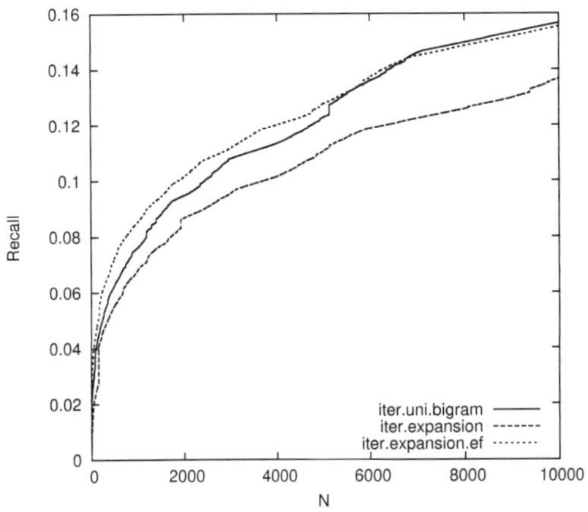

Figure 3: Recall after retrieving N forms for iterative mining on uni- and bigrams, and iterative mining using n-gram expansion with and without using an expansion factor.

Among the longer n-grams in the mining results for the Mediargus corpus, we found many Flemish idiomatic expressions that were not described in the Alpino lexicon. For example:

- had er (AMOUNT) voor veil [had (AMOUNT) for sale]
- (om de muren) van op te lopen [to get terribly annoyed by]
- Ik durf zeggen dat [I dare to say that]
- op punt stellen [to fix/correct something]
- de daver op het lijf [shocked]
- (op) de tippen (van zijn tenen) [being very careful]
- ben fier dat [am proud of]
- Nog voor halfweg [still before halfway]
- (om duimen en vingers) van af te likken [delicious]

Since these expressions are longer than bigrams, they cannot be captured properly without using n-gram expansion. We also found longer n-grams describing valid Dutch phrases that were not described by the grammar or lexicon.

- Het stond in de sterren geschreven dat [It was written in the stars that]
- zowat de helft van de [about half of the]
- er zo goed als zeker van dat [almost sure of]
- laat ons hopen dat het/dit lukt [let us hope that it/this works]

6.3 Scoring methods

The miners that use n-gram expansion perform best with the $M_f = S_f|O_f|$ function, while the other miners perform best with the $M_f = S_f \cdot ln|O_f|$ function. This is not surprising – the iterative miners that do not use n-gram expansion can not make very specific forms and give relatively high scores to forms that happen to occur in unparsable sentences (since some forms in a sentence will have to take blame, if no specific suspicious form is found). If such forms also happen to be frequent, they may be ranked higher than some more suspicious infrequent forms. In the case of the ratio-based miner, there are many forms that are 'suspicious by accident' which may become highly ranked when they are more frequent than very suspicious, but infrequent forms. Since the miners with n-gram expansion can find specific suspicious forms and shift blame to them, there is less chance of accidentally ranking a form to highly by directly including the frequency of observations of that form within unparsable sentences in the scoring function.

6.4 Pattern expansion

We have done some preliminary experiments with pattern expansion, allowing for patterns consisting of words and part of speech tags. For this experiment we trained a Hidden Markov Model part of speech tagger on 90% of the Dutch Eindhoven corpus using a small tag set. We then extracted 50000 unparsable and about 495000 parsable sentences from the Flemish Mediargus corpus. The pattern expansion preprocessor was then used to find interesting patterns.

We give two patterns that were extracted to give an impression how patterns can be useful. A frequent pattern was *doorheen N* (*through* followed by a (proper) noun). In Flemish a sentence such as *We reden met de auto doorheen Frankrijk* (literal: *We drove with the car through France*) is allowed, while in standard Dutch the particle *heen* is separated from the preposition *door*. Consequently, the same sentence in standard Dutch is *We reden met de auto door Frankrijk heen*. Mining on word n-grams provided hints for this difference in Flemish through forms such as *doorheen Krottegem*, *doorheen Engeland*, *doorheen Hawai*, and *doorheen Middelkerke*, but the pattern provides a more general description with a higher frequency.

Another pattern that was found is *wegens Prep Adj* (*because of* followed by a preposition and an adjective). This pattern captures prepositional modifiers where *wegens* is the head, and the following words within the constituent form an argument, such as in the sentence *Dat idee werd snel opgeborgen wegens te duur* (literal: *That idea became soon archived because of too expensive*). This pattern provided a more general description of forms such as *wegens te breed* (*because it is too wide*), *wegens te deprimerend* (*because it is too depressing*), *wegens niet rendabel* (*because it is not profitable*), and *wegens te ondraaglijk* (*because it is too unbearable*).

While instances of both patterns were found using the word n-gram based miner, patterns consolidate different instances. For example, there were 120 forms with a high suspicion containing the word *wegens*. If such a form is corrected, the other examples may still need to be checked to see if a solution to the parsing problem is comprehensive. The pattern gives a more general description of the problem, and as such, most of these 120 forms can be represented by the pattern *wegens Prep Adj*.

Since we are still optimizing the pattern expander to scale to large corpora, we have not performed an automatic evaluation using the Dutch Wikipedia yet.

7 Conclusions

We combined iterative error mining with expansion of forms to n-grams of an arbitrary length, that are long enough to capture interesting phenomena, but not longer. We dealt with the problem of data sparseness by introducing an expansion factor that softens when the expanded form is very frequent.

In addition to the generalization of iterative error mining, we introduced a method for automatic evaluation. This allows us to test modifications to the error miner without going through the tedious task of ranking and judging the results manually.

Using this automatic evaluation method, we have shown that iterative error mining improves upon ratio-based error mining. As expected, adding bigrams improves performance. Allowing expansion beyond bigrams can lead to data sparseness problems, but if we correct for data sparseness the performance of the miner improves over mining on just unigrams and bigrams.

We have also described preliminary work on a preprocessor that allows for more general patterns that incorporate additional information, such as part of speech tags and lemmas. We hope to optimize and improve pattern-based mining in the future and evaluate it automatically on larger corpora.

The error mining methods described in this paper are generic, and can be used for any grammar or parser, as long as the sentences within the corpus can be divided in a list of parsable and unparsable sentences. The error miner is freely available[5], and is optimized to work on large corpora. The source distribution includes a graphical user interface for browsing mining results, showing the associated sentences, and removing forms when they have been corrected in the grammar or lexicon.

References

Gosse Bouma, Gertjan van Noord, and Robert Malouf. 2001. Alpino: Wide-coverage Computational Analysis of Dutch. In *Computational Linguistics in The Netherlands 2000*.

Ann Copestake and Dan Flickinger. 2000. An open source grammar development environment and broad-coverage English grammar using HPSG. In *Proceedings of LREC 2000*, pages 591–600.

Udi Manber and Gene Myers. 1990. Suffix arrays: a new method for on-line string searches. In *SODA '90: Proceedings of the first annual ACM-SIAM symposium on Discrete algorithms*, pages 319–327. Society for Industrial and Applied Mathematics.

Benoît Sagot and Éric de la Clergerie. 2006. Error mining in parsing results. In *ACL-44: Proceedings of the 21st International Conference on Computational Linguistics and the 44th annual meeting of the Association for Computational Linguistics*, pages 329–336, Morristown, NJ, USA. Association for Computational Linguistics.

[5] http://www.let.rug.nl/~dekok/errormining/

Gertjan Van Noord. 2004. Error mining for wide-coverage grammar engineering. In *ACL '04: Proceedings of the 42nd Annual Meeting on Association for Computational Linguistics*, page 446, Morristown, NJ, USA. Association for Computational Linguistics.

C. J. van Rijsbergen. 1979. *Information retrieval*. Butterworths, London, 2 edition.

Author Index